# A Beginner's Guide
# to Scientific Method

P. 55
falsefiability
verifiability

Ch. 5
P. 91

Ch. 6  P 125

# A Beginner's Guide to Scientific Method

## Third Edition

STEPHEN S. CAREY

Portland Community College

WADSWORTH
CENGAGE Learning™

Australia • Brazil • Japan • Korea • Mexico • Singapore • Spain • United Kingdom • United States

**WADSWORTH**
CENGAGE Learning™

**A Beginner's Guide to Scientific Method, Third Edition**
**Stephen S. Carey**

Publisher: Holly J. Allen
Acquisition Editor: Steve Wainwright
Assistant Editor: Lee McCracken
Editorial Assistant: Anna Lustig
Marketing Manager: Worth Hawes
Print/Media Buyer: Doreen Suruki
Permissions Editor: Sarah Harkrader
Production Service: Shepherd, Inc.
Copy Editor: Judith Cartisano
Cover Designer: Belinda Fernandez
Compositor: Shepherd, Inc.

© 2004 Wadsworth, Cengage Learning

For product information and technology assistance, contact us at
**Cengage Learning Customer & Sales Support, 1-800-354-9706**

For permission to use material from this text or product, submit all requests online at
**www.cengage.com/permissions**
Further permissions questions can be emailed to
**permissionrequest@cengage.com**

Library of Congress Control Number: 2002116952

ISBN-13: 978-0-534-58450-4

ISBN-10: 0-534-58450-0

**Wadsworth**
10 Davis Drive
Belmont, CA 94002-3098
USA

Cengage Learning is a leading provider of customized learning solutions with office locations around the globe, including Singapore, the United Kingdom, Australia, Mexico, Brazil, and Japan. Locate your local office at:
**international.cengage.com/region**

Cengage Learning products are represented in Canada by Nelson Education, Ltd.

For your course and learning solutions, visit
**academic.cengage.com**

Purchase any of our products at your local college store or at our preferred online store
**www.ichapters.com**

Printed in Canada
5  6  7  8  9  10  11  10  09  08

# Contents

# Preface

This book is written for the student who has little or no background in the sciences. Its aim is to provide a brief, nontechnical introduction to the basic methods underlying all good scientific research. Though I use this book as the main text in a college level critical thinking course about science and scientific method, it could easily be used as a supplement in any course in which students are required to have some basic understanding of how science is done.

Some will object to the very idea of a basic method underlying all the sciences, on the ground that there is probably nothing common to all good science other than being judged good science. While there is certainly something to this objection, I think there are a few basic procedures to which instances of good scientific research must adhere. If anything deserves to be called the scientific method, it is the simple but profoundly fundamental process wherein new ideas are put to the test—everything from the most rarefied and grand theoretical constructs to the claims of the experimenter to have discovered some new fact about the natural world.

Scientific method rests on the notion that every idea about the workings of nature has consequences and that these consequences provide a basis for testing the idea in question. How this insight is worked out in the world of science is really all this book is about. No doubt, much good science is one step removed from the proposing and testing of new ideas and this is the "something" to the objection above. But whenever science attempts to understand how or why things happen as they do, a basic, underlying methodology generally emerges.

This is not to say that there is a step-by-step recipe which, if followed, will invariably lead to a greater understanding of nature. If I have succeeded at only one thing, I hope it is at showing the tentativeness with which scientific results are issued and the utter openness to revision that is essential to good science.

An essential part of an introduction to anything is an account of what it is not. Hence, roughly a third of the text, in parts of Chapter 2 and 4 and especially in Chapter 6, is about the antithesis of good science—bogus or pseudoscience. Inclusion of material on how not to do science is all the more important since, for the general student, much of the presumed "science" to which he or she will be exposed will be in the form of the rather extravagant claims of the pseudoscientist. To confirm this, one need only turn to the astrology column of any major newspaper or turn on one of the many television programs that purport to provide an objective investigation of the paranormal.

You will find interspersed at strategic points, what I call *quick reviews*—brief summaries of material from chapter subsections. Their purpose is to provide the text with some breathing room but also to encourage the student to stop and reflect on what they have read when they have completed an important topic.

## EXERCISES

Students generally learn by doing, not by talking about doing. Thus, every important idea in the text is an idea with which the student is asked to grapple in solving the chapter exercises. Each chapter ends with a lengthy set of exercises; they are the part of the book of which I am most proud and for which I can claim some originality. I have tried to write exercises that are challenging and fun to think about, require no special expertise, and yet illustrate the extent to which scientific problem solving requires a great deal of creativity. Many of the exercises come not from the world of official science but from ordinary life. This illustrates a theme with which the book opens: Much of what is involved in attempting to do science is thoroughgoing, hardworking common sense, the very best instrument in solving many of the problems of our day-to-day lives.

Many of the exercises are written in a manner that requires the student to work with a number of key ideas all at once. At the end of Chapter 4, for example, the student is asked to solve problems involving all of the ideas discussed in the chapter and a few from earlier chapters as well. The exercises in Chapter 6 rely on ideas from throughout the book. My preference is to introduce students straightaway to the fact that most interesting problems involve a complex of problematic issues, and that problem solving begins with two essential steps: (1) getting a good overall sense of the problem or problems, and (2) only then beginning to break its solution down into a series of discrete bits of critical work.

Exercises in Chapter 4 and Chapter 5 require the student to design some sort of experiment. I have found these exercises particularly useful in encouraging students to think both creatively and critically. I assign different problems to small groups of students as homework to be done as a group. The homework results of each group are then exchanged with another group who must criticize the design submitted by the first group. In class, designers and criticizers meet and refine each of the two experiments on which they have been working. My role in the process is largely to keep the troops calm and to mediate any potentially explosive disputes.

## NEW TO THE THIRD EDITION

New to the third edition is a chapter devoted to observation—Chapter 2. The material on explanations has been divided between two shorter chapters, and extraordinary claims are now covered in Chapter 2 and Chapter 4 rather than in a chapter of their own. The chapter on fallacious applications of scientific method—now Chapter 6—has been reorganized and simplified. Several other minor changes will, I hope, make the ideas presented more accessible to students. A more explicit definition of science and of scientific method is given in Chapter 1, and the latter now provides the basis for the order in which major ideas are covered in the ensuing chapters: observing, proposing, and testing new explanations. The material on designing decisive experimental tests in Chapter 4 is simplified; much of the jargon of older editions is gone, and the very idea of a good test is discussed in something close to ordinary language.

Every exercise set has been refined and all contain at least a few new problems. New exercise sets have been added in Chapter 2 and Chapter 5. A few exercise sets have been shortened to keep the overall number of exercises about the same as in earlier editions.

## ACKNOWLEDGMENTS

Having taken much credit for some innovation in the writing of the chapter exercises, I can claim, on the other hand, little originality for much of the expository material, particularly in the first three chapters of this book. The case study at the center of Chapter 1 will reveal, to those familiar with the philosophy of science, my indebtedness to the work of Carl Hempel, particularly his classic introductory text, *Philosophy of Natural Science*. The central approach and organization of Chapter 5 owes much to Ronald Giere's excellent text, *Understanding Scientific Reasoning*. I have also had the good fortune to receive the advice of several readers of earlier versions of my manuscript, including Davis Baird, University of South Carolina; Stanley Baronett and Todd Jones, University of Nevada, Las Vegas; Brad Dowden, California State University, Sacramento; Jim Kalat, North Carolina State University; and Bonnie Paller, California State University, Northridge. Special thanks to the reviewers of the first, second, and third editions, David Conway, University of Missouri, St. Louis; George Gale, University of Missouri, Kansas City; Judy Obaza, King's College; June Ross, Western Washington University; LaVonne Batalden, Colby Sawyer College; Blinda E. McClelland, University of Texas at Austin; Benjamin B. Steele, Colby-Sawyer College; and Jayne Tristan, University of North Carolina. Nearly every change in the second and third edition was motivated by their advice and suggestions.

One final note. Though my field is philosophy, you will find conspicuously missing any emphasis on central topics in the philosophy of science. There is, for example, no explicit discussion of the hypothetical-deductive method, of the covering law model of explanation, nor of their attendant difficulties, of the rather more notorious problems in the theory of confirmation, nor of the infighting between realists and antirealists. My hunch (which is considerably beneath a firm belief) is that an introduction to anything should avoid philosophical contemplation about the foundations of that thing, lest it lose focus, if not its course, in the sight of its audience. Once the thing in question is fully absorbed and understood, then and only then is it time for philosophical contemplation of its deep commitments. Though I have not altogether avoided topics dear to the philosopher of science, I discuss them briefly and, for the most part, in a jargon-free fashion. My hope is that I have not purchased economy and readability at the expense of either accuracy or a sense of wonder about the philosophical issues embedded in the methods by which science is conducted.

*Stephen S. Carey*

# 1

# Science

Science when well digested is nothing
but good sense and reason.

STANISLAUS

## JUST WHAT IS SCIENCE?

We all have a passing familiarity with the world of science. Rarely does a week go by wherein a new scientific study or discovery is not reported in the media. "Astronomers confirm space structure that's mind-boggling in its immensity," and "Scientists identify gene tied to alcoholism," are the headlines from two recent stories in my daily newspaper. Another opened with the following: "A panel of top scientists has dismissed claims that radiation from electric power lines causes cancer, reproductive disease, and behavioral health problems." Yet many of us would be hard pressed to say much more about the nature of science than that science is whatever it is scientists do for a living. Hardly an illuminating account!

So, what more might we say in response to the question, "Just what is science?" We cannot hope to answer this question by looking at the subject matter of the sciences. Science investigates natural phenomena of every conceivable sort—from the physical to the biological to the social. Scientists study everything from events occurring at the time of the formation of the universe to the stages of human intellectual and emotional development to the migratory patterns of butterflies. Though in what follows we will often refer to "nature" or "the natural world" as that which science investigates, we must understand that the "world" of the scientist includes much more than our planet and its inhabitants. Judging by its subject matter, then, science is the study of very nearly everything.

Nor can we hope to answer our question by looking at the range of activities in which scientists engage. Scientists theorize about things, organize vast research projects, build equipment, dig up relics, take polls, and run experiments on everything from people to protons to plants. A description of science in terms of the sorts of things scientists typically do, then, is not going to tell us much about the nature of science, for there does not seem to be anything scientists typically do.

If we are to understand just what science is, we must look at science from a different perspective. We must ask ourselves, first, why scientists study the natural world, and, then we must look at the way in which scientific enquiry is conducted, no matter what its subject.

*understanding science w/o the science references*

## ASKING WHY

Of course, we cannot hope to give a simple, ubiquitous reason why each and every scientist studies the natural world. There are bound to be as many reasons as there are practicing scientists. Nevertheless, there is a single "why" underlying all scientific research. In general, scientists study the natural world to figure out why things happen as they do. We all know, for example, that the moon is riddled with craters. From a scientific point of view, what is of real interest is precisely why this should be so. What natural processes have led to the formation of the craters? At the most basic level, then, science can be defined by reference to this interest in figuring things out. So, an essential part of the answer to our question. "Just what is science?" involves the basic aim of science. *Science is that activity, the underlying aim of which is to further our understanding of why things happen as they do in the natural world.* To see what it is that scientists do in attempting to "make sense" of nature, let's take a look at an historical instance that, as it turns out, played an important role in the development of modern medicine.

Up until the middle of the nineteenth century, little was known about the nature of infectious diseases and the ways in which they are transmitted. In the mid-eighteen hundreds, however, an important clue emerged from the work of a Viennese doctor, Ignaz Semmelweis. At the time, many pregnant women who entered Vienna General Hospital died shortly after having given birth. Their deaths were attributed to something called "childbed fever." Curiously, the death rate from childbed fever in the hospital ward where the patients were treated by physicians was five time higher than in another ward where women were seen only by midwives. Physicians were at a loss to explain why this should be so. But then something remarkable occurred. One of Semmelweis's colleagues cut his finger on a scalpel that had been used during an autopsy. Within days, the colleague exhibited symptoms remarkably like those associated with childbed fever and shortly thereafter died. Semmelweis knew that physicians often spent time with students in the autopsy room prior to visiting their patients in the maternity ward.

Thanks largely to the clue provided by the death of his colleague, Semmelweis speculated that something like the following might be responsible for the glaring differences in death rates in the two wards. Childbed fever was caused by something that physicians came into contact with in the autopsy room and then inadvertently transmitted to pregnant women during the course of their rounds in the maternity ward. Semmelweis appropriately termed this something, "cadaveric matter."

The challenge faced by Semmelweis was to devise a way of testing his ideas about the link between cadaveric matter and childbed fever. Semmelweis reasoned as follows: If childbed fever is caused by cadaveric matter transmitted from physician to patient, and if something were done to eradicate all traces of cadaveric matter from the physicians prior to their visiting patients in the maternity ward, then the incidence of childbed fever should diminish. In fact, Semmelweis arranged for physicians to wash their hands and arms in chlorinated lime water—a powerful cleansing agent—prior to their rounds in the maternity ward. Within two years, the death rate from childbed fever in the ward attended by physicians approached that of the ward attended by midwives. By 1848, Semmelweis was losing not a single women to childbed fever!

## SCIENTIFIC METHOD

At its most basic level, scientific method is a simple, three-step process by which scientists investigate nature. Begin by carefully observing some aspect of nature. If something emerges that is not well understood, speculate about its explanation and then find some way to test those speculations. Each step—observing, explaining, and testing—is nicely illustrated by the historical event we have just described.

### Observing

Before we can begin to think about the explanation for something we must make sure we have a clear sense of the facts surrounding the phenomenon we are investigating. Semmelweis's explanation of childbed fever was prompted by a number of facts, each the product of careful observation: First, the fact that the rates of childbed fever differed in the wards in question; second, that patients in the ward where the rate was the highest were treated by physicians, not midwives; and finally the remarkable symptoms of his dying colleague.

Getting at the facts can both help us to establish the need for a new explanation and provide clues as to what it might involve. Suppose, for example, that careful long-term observation revealed to Semmelweis that on average the death rates were about the same in the two wards. In some months or years the rate was higher in one ward, in others, higher in the other. In these circumstances nothing puzzling needs to be accounted for—the original set of observations would seem to be nothing more than the sort of brief statistical fluctuation that is bound to occur now and then in any long series of events. But as Semmelweis found, the difference in death rates was not a momentary aberration. Thus, by careful observation Semmelweis was able to establish that something not fully understood was going on. It was Semmelweis's good fortune to then make the key observation that suggested what might be responsible for the problem—the unusual similarity between the symptoms of the dying mothers and his sick colleague.

## Proposing Explanations

To explain something is to introduce a set of factors that account for how or why the thing in question has come to be the case. Why, for example, does the sun rise and set daily? The explanation is that the earth rotates about its axis every twenty-four hours. When something is not well understood, its explanation will be unclear. Hence the first step in trying to make sense of a puzzling set of facts is to propose what we might call an explanatory story—a set of conjectures that would, if true, account for the puzzle. And this is precisely what Semmelweis set about doing. Semmelweis's explanatory story involved the claims that something in cadaveric matter causes childbed fever and that this something can be transmitted from cadaver to physician to patient by simple bodily contact.

Semmelweis's explanation was all the more interesting because it introduced notions that were at the time themselves quite new and puzzling—some very new and controversial ideas about the way in which disease is transmitted. Many of Semmelweis's contemporaries, for example, believed that childbed fever was the result of an epidemic, like the black plague, that somehow infected only pregnant women. Others suspected that dietary problems or difficulties in the general care of the women were to blame. Thus, in proposing his explanation, Semmelweis hinted at the existence of a new set of explanatory factors that challenged the best explanations of the day, and which had the potential to challenge prevailing views about how diseases are spread. All that remained for Semmelweis was to find a way to test his explanation.

## Testing Explanations

How can we determine whether a proposed explanation is correct or mistaken? By the following strategy. First, we look for a consequence of the explanation—something that ought to occur, if circumstances are properly arranged and if the explanation is on the right track. Then we carry out an experiment designed to determine whether the predicted result actually will occur under these circumstances. If we get the results we have predicted, we have good reason to believe our explanation is right. If we fail to get them, we have some initial reason to suspect we may be wrong or, at the very least, that we may need to modify the proposed explanation.

This was precisely the strategy Semmelweis employed in testing his ideas about the cause of childbed fever. If something physicians have come into contact with prior to entering the maternity ward is causing the problem and if this "something" is eradicated, then it follows that the rate of childbed fever should drop. And, indeed, once these circumstances were arranged, the outcome predicted by Semmelweis occurred. As a result, he was confident that his initial hunch was on the right track. By contrast, had there been no reduction in the rate of childbed fever as a result of the experiment, Semmelweis would at least have had a strong indication that his hunch was mistaken.

At the most basic level, the scientific method is nothing more than the simple three-step process we have just illustrated—carefully observing some aspect of nature, proposing and then testing possible explanations for those observational findings that are not well understood. In the chapters to follow we will need to add a great deal of detail to our initial sketch of scientific method. We will come to recognize that scientific method is not all that straightforward nor, for that matter, easy to apply. Explanations are not always as readily tested as our initial examples might suggest nor are test results always as decisive as we might like them to be. We will also find that, with some minor variations, scientific method can be used to test interesting and controversial claims as well as explanations. For now, however, we can use what we have discovered about scientific method to get at the remainder of the answer to our opening question.

Just what is science? *Science is that activity, the underlying aim of which is to further our understanding of why things happen as they do in the natural world. It accomplishes this goal by applications of scientific method—the process of observing nature, isolating a facet that is not well understood, and then proposing and testing possible explanations.*

## THE CONSEQUENCES OF SCIENCE

Before moving on, an important caveat is in order. In focusing on the preoccupation of science with making sense of nature—of providing and testing explanations—we have ignored what is surely an equally compelling interest of the sciences, namely, making the world a better place to live via technological innovation. Indeed, when we think of science, we often think of it in terms of some of its more spectacular applications: computers, high speed trains and jets, nuclear reactors, microwave ovens, new vaccines, etc. Yet, our account of what is involved in science is principally an account of science at the theoretical level, not at the level of application to technological problems.

Don't be misled by our use of the term "theoretical" here. Theories are often thought of as little more than guesses or hunches about things. In this sense, if we have a theory about something, we have at most a kind of baseless conjecture about the thing. In science, however, "theory" has a related though different meaning. Scientific theories may be tentative, and at a certain point in their development will involve a fair amount of guesswork. But what makes a scientific theory a theory is its ability to explain, not the fact that at some point in its development it may contain some rather questionable notions. Much as there will be tentative, even imprecise, explanations in science, so also will there be secure, well established explanations. Thus, when we distinguish between theory and application in science we are contrasting two essential concerns of science: concern with understanding nature, and concern with exploiting that theoretical understanding as a means of solving rather more practical, technological problems.

Yet there is an important, if by now obvious, connection between the worlds of theoretical and applied science. With very few exceptions, technical innovation springs from theoretical understanding. The scientists who designed, built, and tested the first nuclear reactors, for example, depended heavily on a great deal of prior theoretical and experimental work on the structure of the atom and the ways in which atoms of various sorts interact. Similarly, as the case we have been discussing should serve to remind us, simple but effective new procedures for preventing the spread of disease were possible only after the theoretical work of Semmelweis and others began to yield some basic insight into the nature of germs and the ways in which diseases are spread.

## SCIENTIFIC METHOD IN DAILY LIFE

The brief sketch of scientific method given above may have a familiar ring to it and for good reason. To a large extent thinking about things from a scientific perspective—thinking about the "hows" and "whys" of things—involves nothing more than the kind of problem solving we do in our daily lives.

To see this, imagine the following case. For the last few nights, you haven't been sleeping well. You've had a hard time getting to sleep and have begun waking up frequently during the course of the night. This is unusual, for you are normally a sound sleeper. What could be causing the problem? Well, next week is final exam week and you have been staying up late every evening, studying. Could concern about your upcoming exams be causing the problem? This seems unlikely, since you have been through exam week several times before and have had no problems sleeping. Is there anything else unusual about your behavior in the last few nights? It has been quite warm, so you have been consuming large quantities of your favorite drink, iced tea, while studying. And this could explain the problem. For you are well aware that most teas contain a stimulant, caffeine. It may well be the caffeine in your iced tea that is disturbing your sleep! But is this the right explanation? Here, a relatively quick, easy, and effective test can be performed. You might, for example, try drinking ice water instead of iced tea in the evening. If you were to do this, and if you again began sleeping normally, we would have good reason to think that our explanation was right; it must be the caffeine in the iced tea. Moreover, if you were not to begin sleeping normally we would have some reason to suspect that we have not yet found the right explanation; eliminating the caffeine didn't seem to do the trick.

Though nothing of any great scientific consequence turns on the solution of our little puzzle, the solution nevertheless is a straightforward application of scientific method: observing something unusual, venturing a guess as to what its explanation might be, and then finding a way to test that guess.

# THINGS TO COME

In the chapters to follow, our central concern with be to expand the preliminary sketch of scientific method given so far. Along the way, we will pay particular attention to the pitfalls scientists are likely to encounter in making accurate observations and in designing and carrying out decisive experimental tests. On our agenda will be a number of controversial topics, perhaps none more so than the distinction between legitimate and fraudulent applications of scientific method. Nothing can do more to lend an air of credibility to a claim than the suggestion that it has been "proven in scientific studies" or that it is "backed by scientific evidence." A sad fact, however, is that many claims made in the name of science are founded on gross misapplications of some aspect of scientific method. Indeed, so numerous are the ways in which scientific method can be abused that we will find it necessary to devote a chapter to fallacies commonly committed under the guise of scientific research.

Our goals, then, in the chapters to follow are twofold. Our first and most important goal is to become familiar with the basic methodology common to all good scientific research. Our second goal is to learn to distinguish between legitimate and bogus applications of scientific method. Having accomplished these goals, I think you will find yourself quite capable of thinking clearly and critically about the claims of scientists and charlatans alike to have advanced our understanding of the world about us.

# EXERCISES

*Try your hand at telling explanatory stories. The following exercises all describe curious things. See if you can come up with one or two explanations for each. Keep in mind, your explanation need not be true but it must be such that it would explain the phenomena in question, if it were true.*

1. A survey done recently revealed that whereas 10 percent of all 20-year-olds are left-handed, only about 2 percent of all 75-year-olds are left-handed.

2. Have you ever noticed that baseball players tend to be quite superstitious? Batters and pitchers alike often run through a series of quite bizarre gestures before every pitch.

3. Americans have a serious weight problem. In the last decade, both the number of Americans who are overweight and who are clinically obese has increased by more than 10 percent. The increase over the last two decades in both is nearly 20 percent.

4. Why have so many Americans switched from driving sedans to sports utility vehicles and trucks in the last few years?

5. We all know what happens when we depress the handle on a toilet. The flapper inside the tank opens and water rushes into the bowl, flushing it out and refilling the bowl. But what keeps the fresh water in the bowl?

# 2

# Observation

## MAKING ACCURATE OBSERVATIONS

Suppose you were to pause for a few minutes and try to list all of the objects in your immediate vicinity. You would quickly realize that the task of making a set of accurate observations can be a tricky business. In this case, one problem stems from the fact that it is not all that clear what qualifies as an object nor, for that matter, what it is to be in the immediate vicinity. The book you are reading is undoubtedly an object. But what of the bookmark stuck between its pages? No doubt the picture on the wall qualifies. But what of the nail on which it is hanging? And how should we fix the limits of the immediate vicinity? Do we mean by this the room in which you are sitting? Everything within a 10-foot circumference of you? Everything within reaching distance? Even after we have settled on working definitions for these key terms, we face an additional problem. Doubtless you are likely to miss a few things on your first visual sweep. So we need to find some way to guarantee that we have included everything that fits in our two categories.

In general, the process of making a set of observations must be sensitive to a number of concerns, two of which are illustrated in the case above.

1. Do we have a clear sense of what the relevant phenomena are?

2. Have we found a way to insure we have not overlooked anything in the process of making our observations?

These two questions can usually be addressed in a fairly straightforward way. Some careful thinking about just how key terms are to be applied will settle the first. Keeping a written record of our results will satisfy the second. In the example above, one simple way to accomplish this would be to make a list of the objects found in a first set of observations and then add in overlooked items from a second set. Another would be to ask someone else to check your results. The need for a written record is all the more crucial because of the natural temptation to think we can do without one. Try, for example, to think how many times today you have done something commonplace like, say, sitting down or opening your wallet or saying "hello." Recollection will undoubtedly turn up a number of instances. But our memories are fallible and we are likely to miss something no matter how confident we are that we have remembered all the relevant cases. The solution is simply to keep some sort of written tally.

Observations are not always undertaken with a clear sense of what data may be relevant. Think, for example, of a detective at the scene of a crime. What small details need to be noted or perhaps preserved for future reference? Moreover, a set of observations may yield unanticipated information—data that does not conform to the observer's sense of what is relevant—but information that is nonetheless of some importance. Recently, medical researchers at a large university were studying the effect of calcium on pregnancy-related high blood pressure. Though they observed no significant reductions in the blood pressure of the women in their study who took calcium, they did notice something quite interesting and unexpected. The women in their study who took calcium during pregnancy had lower rates of depression than those who took a placebo instead of calcium. As a result, the researchers began an entirely new study, one designed to determine the extent to which calcium can prevent depression in pregnant women. As this example suggests, it is important not to become too attached to fixed notions of what may constitute relevant observational data. Otherwise, we run the risk of missing something that may turn out to be significant.

Often in science, a set of observations will be prompted by the need to learn more about something that is not well understood. Not too long ago, for example, researchers uncovered what seemed to be a curious fact. On average, right-handed people live longer than left-handed people.[1] To begin to understand why this is the case we would need to search carefully for factors that affect only the left-handed (or right-handed), and which might account for the different mortality rates of the two groups. When, as in this case, observations involve phenomena that are not well understood, three additional concerns may need to be addressed.

3. What do we know for sure? What is based on fact and what on conjecture or assumption?

4. Have we considered any necessary comparative information?

5. Have our observations been contaminated by expectation or belief?

Rarely will the answers to these questions come easily or quickly. Consider what may be involved in dealing with each.

---

**BOX 2.1 How Good Are Your Powers of Observation?**

We observe things every day that we scarcely notice. How many of the following questions can you answer?

1. In which direction do revolving doors turn?
2. When you walk, do your arms swing with or against the rhythm of your legs?
3. What are the five colors on a Campbell's soup label?
4. In which direction do pieces travel around a Monopoly board, clockwise or counterclockwise?
5. On the American flag, is the uppermost stripe red or white?
6. In Grant Wood's painting "American Gothic," is the man to the viewer's left or right?
7. In which hand does the Statue of Liberty hold her torch?
8. Which side of a woman's blouse has the buttonholes on it—from her view?
9. How many sides are there on a standard pencil?
10. On most traffic lights, is the green light on the top or the bottom?

Answers are given at the end of the chapter.

---

*What do we know for sure? What is based on fact and what on conjecture or assumption?* Have you ever noticed that the full moon often appears appreciably larger when it is near the horizon? As you read this you are probably picturing a large, yellow-orangish moon in your mind's eye. You've probably also heard others comment on this phenomenon. But appearances can be deceiving, opinions wrong. In fact the moon is not appreciably larger when near the horizon. This can be determined by a simple set of observations. The next time the moon seems unusually large, stretch your arm as far as it will go and use your thumb to measure the moon's diameter. Make a note of how big it seems and then make a similar measurement when the moon is overhead and apparently much smaller. You will find that its diameter is about the same in both cases. What makes the moon appear larger in the former case is its close proximity to other objects near the horizon. When we judge the size of the moon by reference to other objects—objects not near the moon when it is overhead—we mistakenly conclude that its image is larger.

As this example illustrates, it is always worthwhile to pause and think about any assumptions we may be making about the phenomenon under investigation. Don't let unwarranted assumption masquerade as fact. Always ask: What do I really know about the phenomenon under investigation and what am I assuming based on what I have been told or have heard, read, etc.? The answer to this question may point you in the direction of observations you will need to make to test whatever assumptions you have unearthed.

Jim Hightower, a well known political writer, recalls that as a child he was told by his grandfather that raccoons always wash their food because they do not have salivary glands. But after spending an early morning observing a family of raccoons he quickly came to realize that what his grandfather had told him—what he assumed to be true—was in error. The raccoons didn't wash the food he left for them before eating it, and appeared to be salivating. As it turns out raccoons do have salivary glands. Often, it seems, we can sort fact from fiction simply by taking time to look and see what is going on rather than implicitly trusting whatever assumptions we may bring to the investigation.

*Have we considered any necessary comparative information?* Many people claim that strange things happen when the moon is full. One interesting and curious claim is that more babies are born on days when the moon is full or nearly full than during any other time of the month. What observations would we need to make to determine whether there is anything to this claim? Certainly we would want to look at the data pertaining to the number of births when the moon is full. But this is only part of the story. We would also need to look at the numbers for other times, times when the moon is not full. If the birth rate is not appreciably higher when the moon is full, then there is little remarkable about the claim at issue. Lots of births occur when the moon is full. But then lots of births occur during all phases of the moon. Indeed, careful studies done at a number of hospitals reveal that there is nothing unusual about the birth rate when the moon is full. When birth rates were examined over the period of a year or two, it turned out that, on average, there were no more or less births during the period near a full moon than during any other period. In a given month, there might be a few more (or less) births near a full moon than during other parts of the month, but when averaged out over a long period of time, the difference disappears.

You've probably heard that apparently infertile couples who adopt a child frequently go on to give birth to a child. Is there some connection between the two events? To get at the answer to this question, we need comparative data. How, generally, do such couples fare when compared with another group of couples—those who are diagnosed as being infertile but choose not to adopt? (We might also want to look at what happens to fertile couples who do and do not adopt as well.) As it turns out, pregnancy rates for apparently infertile couples who do not adopt are about the same as for similar couples who adopt.

As these examples suggest, part of the point of making a set of observations is to determine what, if anything, is unusual about the data collected. Remember, the business of science is understanding. Thus, it is crucial to determine whether a set of observations present us with something that is not well understood. As we have seen, there is nothing out of the ordinary about the number of births when the moon is full nor about the pregnancy rates of infertile couples; in neither case have we uncovered anything that requires explanation. The process of making observations should always be undertaken with an eye to figuring out whether the results square with what is currently known. And this often involves hunting for the right sort of comparative data—data that will enable us to decide the extent to which our observations have led us to something that really does need explaining.

*Have our observations been contaminated by expectation or belief?* Our experiences are colored by our beliefs and expectations. When I hear a chirping sound on the ledge outside my office, I assume that what I am hearing is a bird, largely because of prior experiences, the beliefs formulated on the basis of those experiences, and other relevant background beliefs. In the past when I have heard chirping outside my window I have looked out and observed a jay or a robin. And so I make the easy and entirely unproblematic inference that I am now hearing a robin or a jay though, strictly speaking, what I am hearing is only a noise that sounds to me like chirping.

The extent to which beliefs can influence our experiences is powerfully illustrated in the following example. Read the passage below and before reading on, pause and try to figure out what it is about.

> With hocked gems financing him, our hero bravely defied all scornful laughter that tried to prevent his scheme. "Your eyes deceive," he had said. "An egg, not a table correctly typifies this unexplored planet." Now three sturdy sisters sought proof. Forging along, sometimes through calm vastness, yet more often very turbulent peaks and valleys, days became weeks as many doubters spread fearful rumors about the edge. At last from nowhere welcome winged creatures appeared, signifying momentous success.

If you are like me, you found this passage hard to decipher and would find it equally difficult to give a rough paraphrase of what it says. In fact, this story is about Columbus's voyage to the Americas. Reread the passage in light of this new information and note how much sense it makes. Obviously, nothing in the passage has changed. What has altered your experience of reading the passage is a new belief about it.

Normally, we do not need to be too concerned with the influence exerted by expectation and belief over our experience. Many, perhaps most of our beliefs are well founded and our expectations usually reliable. Nonetheless, it is important to be aware of the extent to which our observations can be influenced by belief and expectation. The point of making a set of scientific observations is to come up with an objective record of what is going on, often in circumstances where we are really not sure. When experience is processed through the filter of belief and expectation, distortion can creep into our account of what we are observing, particularly when we have strong convictions about how things are going to turn out. Several years ago, for example, some people claimed that the word "sex" could be discerned in a puff of smoke in a brief sequence from the Walt Disney film, *The Lion King*. I have shown the sequence to hundreds of students. Most of those who have not heard that "sex" is in the puff of smoke simply do not see it. However, once they are told what to look for, many people can see the word though many still do not. Seeing is believing, but in this case it seems what one believes can determine what one sees!

Trained scientists are not immune to the influence of expectation and belief on observation. In 1877 and 1881, the Italian astronomer, Giovanni Schiaparelli, turned his telescope to Mars, which was unusually close to earth. Schiaparelli claimed that he had observed *canali* on the surface of the planet. Reports of this event in the English-speaking media translated the Italian *canali* as "canals" though the word means both "canals" and "channels," the latter meaning being intended by Schiaparelli. Schiaparelli had observed straight lines arranged in a complex fashion but which he did not take to be unequivocal evidence of intelligent beings on Mars. A number of astronomers, among them the American Percival Lowell, claimed also to see Martian "canals," some going so far as to draw detailed maps of them. (At the time, astronomical photography was not sufficiently developed to allow for pictures of Mars. The "canals" were observed visually, a fact that allowed for a good deal of leeway in interpreting what was observed.) Of course, there are no canals on Mars. Those astronomers who believed that they were seeing canals were victims of the influence belief can exert over observation.

An even more remarkable example of the extent to which belief can influence scientific observation involves a long since discredited phenomenon, N-rays. Several years after the discovery of X-rays in the late 1800s, a highly respected French physicist, René Blondlot, announced that he had detected a subtle new form of radiation, N-rays, named after the University of Nancy, where he was a professor. The evidence for the new form of radiation was provided by changes in the intensity of a spark when jumping a gap between two wires running from a cathode ray tube, the forerunner of the modern TV tube. In subsequent experiments, Blondlot discovered that the effects of N-rays were the most pronounced for very weak and short sparks and that they could be refracted by a prism, something not true of X-rays. The problem was that other experimenters had mixed results in trying to replicate Blondlot's experiments. Some confirmed his findings, others had no luck. One researcher, Auguste Charpentier, claimed to have evidence that N-rays are emitted by people and animals. The main problem faced by researchers was that the effects of N-rays were quite subtle, involving only slight variations in light intensity. Some critics claimed that the effects could be attributed to the way the human eye reacts to faint light sources. Against his critics, Blondlot and his colleagues insisted they had demonstrated the existence of a new form of radiation, even going so far as to suggest that people not properly trained to observe N-rays would have difficulty detecting them. Matters came to a head in 1905 when an American physicist, Robert Wood, came to Nancy to observe Blondlot's work. One crucial experiment was intended to demonstrate the deflection of N-rays by a prism. Wood asked Blondlot to repeat the experiment but, unbeknownst to Blondlot, removed the prism from the apparatus. Blondlot claimed to obtain the same quantitative measurements of N-ray deflection by the prism even when the prism was missing! Wood published the results of his investigations and within a few years, N-ray research had come to an end. The researchers who for several years provided experimental backing for Blondlot's new phenomenon had simply allowed belief and expectation to contaminate their findings.

The cases we have considered in this section suggest that it is always worthwhile to step back from a set of observations and gain some much needed critical perspective by asking the following. *What am I actually seeing, hearing, etc., and what am I bringing to my observation via the filter of belief and expectation?* Two

---

**QUICK REVIEW 2.1**   Questions to Ponder When Making Observations

---

Do you have a clear sense of what the relevant phenomena are?

Have you found a way to correct for anything that may have been overlooked?

What do you know for sure? What is based on fact and what on conjecture or assumption?

Have you considered any necessary comparative data?

Have your beliefs and expectations influenced your observations?

---

features common to much scientific observation can play an important role in correcting for the influence of belief and expectation. These are the use of instruments to heighten and supplement the senses and the use of quantitative measures to describe and record observations. Instruments like telescopes, microscopes, and medical imaging devices can provide access to phenomena that could not be observed if we were to rely on our senses alone. But they can serve the additional purpose of providing an objective record of what is actually observed. So, for example, a photographic record of the surface of Mars, something not possible at the time of the "discovery" of the canals, led to the final demise of the idea of Martian canals. Simple instruments like the balance scale and the meter stick often enable scientists to provide a quantitative account of their observations. Suppose that the students in one of my classes strike me as being unusually tall. This observation can be put on a more objective footing by the simple expedient of measuring each student and then comparing the results with the measurements of students in other classes. As you are no doubt aware, numbers—mathematics—are often used by scientists. (Indeed, as we will see in Chapter 5, one area of mathematics—the study of probability and statistical inference—is an indispensable tool in the study of causal relationships.) This is because numerical measures permit a more precise description of many sorts of phenomena than would otherwise be possible, as our last example suggests.

## ANOMALOUS PHENOMENA

Accurate observation is especially crucial in science when the phenomena under investigation appears to be *anomalous*. An **anomaly** is something, some state of affairs, that does not square with current, received ways of understanding nature. In 1989 two chemists, Martin Fleischmann and Stanley Pons, announced the results of a series of experiments in which they claimed to have produced nuclear fusion at room temperature. This discovery, if true, had the potential to supply limitless quantities of inexpensive, clean energy. But "cold fusion," as this phenomenon came to be called, presented the scientific community with a real anomaly. Nuclear fusion is a well-known phenomenon; it is the source of the sun's energy, and fusion reactions have been created under laboratory conditions. But for the nuclei of atoms to fuse, temperatures in excess of 10 million degrees are required. One byproduct of fusion is the emission of radiation. Yet Pons and Fleischmann claimed to have observed fusion at a considerably lower temperature and claimed also to have detected very little radiation. The number of neutrons—one major source of radiation—they reported seeing was at least a million times too small to account for the fusion energy they claimed to have produced. If Pons and Fleischmann were right, much of what physicists have discovered about the nature of atomic nuclei and the conditions under which nuclei will fuse would have to be revised if not jettisoned altogether.[2]

Anomalous phenomena play a central role in the evolution of scientific ideas. Such phenomena can provide a way of testing the limits of our current understanding of how nature works and can suggest new and fruitful areas for scientific investigation. For example, in a short period of time near the beginning of the twentieth century, three totally unexpected discoveries were made: X-rays, radioactivity, and the electron. Each challenged conventional views about the structure and behavior of the atom and led within a few years to a much richer understanding of the basic structure of matter. Similarly, the case discussed in Chapter 1—Semmelweis's discovery of "cadaveric matter"—pointed medical science in the direction of a new way of thinking about disease by introducing the then quite startling notion of microorganisms.

No episode from the history of science illustrates the revolutionary impact of anomalous phenomena more powerfully than the discoveries made by Charles Darwin during a five-year sea voyage in the 1830s. Darwin was appointed naturalist on the H.M.S. Beagle, a British navy survey vessel, for a trip that would circle the world in the southern hemisphere. During the voyage Darwin made numerous observations of the various habitats he visited and collected many zoological and botanical species. While visiting the Cape Verde Islands off the coast of Africa he noted that various species of birds resembled species found on the nearby African continent. Later in the voyage Darwin made a series of careful observations of the species inhabiting the small islands of the Galapagos, off the coast of South America. He noted that each island had its own distinct populations of various animals and birds. Darwin made special note of the varieties of finches that inhabited the islands. In particular, he observed that the beaks of finches found on each island varied slightly from those on other islands. His diary contains detailed sketches of these differences along with an account of the tasks these variations enabled the birds to do given the peculiarities of their environment. Moreover, Darwin was surprised to find that similarities between the species inhabiting the Cape Verde and Galapagos Islands were much less striking than those he found between those inhabiting the Cape Verde Islands and Africa. At the time, Darwin did not fully understand the significance of his findings. In a letter written from South America in 1834 Darwin said, "I have not one clear idea about cleavage, lines of upheaval. I have no books which tell me much, and what they do I cannot apply to what I see. In consequence, I draw my own conclusions, and most gloriously ridiculous ones they are." But within five years of his return home Darwin had in place the major pieces of a theory about the gradual development of diversity among living things. (*The Origin of Species,* Darwin's full-blown account of the theory, was not published for another twenty years.) The observations Darwin so painstakingly carried out on his five-year voyage both provided a challenge to the traditional view that all life fits into preestablished, fixed categories, and suggested a revolutionary new mechanism that has since become the cornerstone of the modern biological sciences: evolution by natural selection.

New findings in science need not be as revolutionary as the examples we have considered to challenge conventional thinking. Many anomalies suggest the need for small, incremental changes to prevailing theory. A recent article in the science section of my local newspaper tells of the discovery that prehistoric cave paintings in southern France are much older than previously believed. Radiocarbon dating reveals that some of the paintings are about 30,000 years old. Previous estimates had suggested that such paintings were done sometime between 12,000 to 17,000 years ago. This finding suggests that current ideas about when humans developed "fairly sophisticated artistic talents" will need to be revised. Another story from the same day's paper reports on a new genetic analysis of chimpanzees living in three western African communities. Previous studies had suggested that female chimpanzees have frequent sexual liaisons with males from other communities. The new study, which examined the DNA of the female's offspring, revealed that nearly all offspring were fathered by males from within the females' community. At the very least, these new findings suggest that our current understanding of chimpanzee social structures will need to undergo some revision. Small discoveries like these and their attendant anomalies are commonplace in the day-to-day business of doing science, but their importance should not be underestimated. The challenges they pose to prevailing ideas are the clues required if scientific understanding is to expand.

Anomalies are not the exclusive province of science. Many people claim to have witnessed or to be able to do extraordinary things, things which are at odds with conventional scientific thinking. Some people claim to be able to see colorful "auras" emanating from the human body and to be able to discern things about the character of a person by careful study of these "auric emanations." Others claim to have been contacted by extraterrestrials or to have seen alien space craft—UFOs—hovering in the night sky. Astrologers claim to be able to predict things about your future based on the position of the planets at the time of your birth. Similar claims are made by people who read palms, tea leaves, and tarot cards. Many people claim to have psychic ability of one sort or another: to be able to "see" the future, to read the minds of others, and to manipulate objects by sheer mind power. People claim to have seen ghosts, poltergeists, and assorted cryptozoological creatures—everything from Bigfoot to the Loch Ness Monster. Many claim to have lived past lives and to have left their bodies during near death encounters. Others claim to have communicated with the spirits of long-dead people.

Many extraordinary claims involve healing and medicine. Some dentists claim we are being poisoned by the mercury in our fillings. Iridologists claim to be able to diagnose illness by examining nothing more than the iris of the human eye. Faith healers claim to be able to cure all sorts of illness and disability by prayer and the laying on of hands. Psychic surgeons claim they can perform operations without the use of anesthetic or surgical instruments.

All of these claims have several things in common. First, all are highly controversial, in the sense that though there is some evidence for the truth of each, the evidence is sketchy at best. Second, all appear to be at odds with some aspect of our current understanding of the natural world even though the claims generally do not emerge from mainstream science. Finally, advocates of such claims are often unaware of the extent to which their beliefs are in disagreement with established scientific theory.

Suppose, for example, someone claims to be able to levitate. This claim is controversial precisely in that though there is actually some evidence for levitation—photographs and the apparently sincere testimony of people who claim to have levitated—the evidence is limited. Moreover, if levitation is possible then our current understanding of how and where gravity operates will have to be revised unless we are prepared to postulate some hitherto undiscovered force of sufficient magnitude to counteract gravity.

Or consider the claim, made by many psychics, to be able to divine the future. The evidence for such an ability is scant—in most cases a few clear and correct predictions accompanied by lots of vague and downright wrong ones. Yet if it is the case that some people can "see" what has yet to happen, we must rethink our current view about the nature of causation. Common sense, if nothing else, suggests that if A is the cause of B, then A must occur before B can occur. Yet if the future can be seen, effects can be established long before their causes come into existence. Thus, if the future can be foretold, something somewhere is wrong with our current view of causation.

## OBSERVATION AND ANOMALOUS PHENOMENA

Special care must be taken in investigating anomalies. Something that strikes us as anomalous is something we do not fully understand, and so we may not know precisely what we should be looking for in our initial observations. When, for example, the first cases of what later came to be known as AIDS were reported in the late 1970s, medical researchers knew very little about what they were facing. A particular group of people—gay men in the U.S. and Sweden and heterosexuals in Tanzania and Haiti—began showing remarkably similar symptoms. By 1980 a significant number were dying and by 1981 an alarming number of cases of a rare cancer—Kaposi's sarcoma—were appearing in otherwise healthy gay men. Beyond this, little was known. The extent and nature of the epidemic were unclear and no one had a real clue as to what the cause or causes might be. Moreover, the progression of the disease through the populations it affected did not square well with what was believed about the spread of infectious disease. Years of careful observations, many involving factors that turned out to have no bearing on the problem, were required before the first, tentative picture of the extent and nature of the AIDS epidemic began to emerge.

Anomalies are puzzling and unfamiliar and they are potentially revolutionary as well. If an anomaly can be documented, something has to give. Accepted ideas need to be revised and new forms of explanation may need to be developed and tested. Because so much is at stake, the investigation of anomalies must be undertaken with two goals in mind. The first, of course, is to uncover the facts, to get a sense of what is going on. The second is to determine whether the phenomenon can be "explained away." Can the phenomenon be accounted for by reference to familiar, conventional modes of explanation? Only if conventional explanation fails can we be confident we have uncovered something that is genuinely anomalous. When confronted with an apparent anomaly, most scientists will immediately try to deflate the air of mystery surrounding the phenomenon. So, for example, within days of the first reports of cold fusion, many physicists began to suspect that Pons and Fleischmann's results could be explained in a way that did not involve nuclear fusion. And as things turned out, they were right. The excess heat energy produced in their experiments was the product of a well understood chemical, not nuclear, reaction. This sort of response when confronted with an apparent anomaly is not, as is sometimes suggested, the product of an inability on the part of mainstream scientists to cope with anything that challenges orthodox views. It is, rather, the first necessary step in determining whether something is genuinely anomalous.

In investigating purported anomalies, then, we need to look for clues as to what is going on, but also for clues that suggest that the phenomenon can be explained within the framework of conventional, established methods of explanation. Several years ago, a resident of Seattle, Washington, commented in a letter to the editor of the city's major daily newspaper that something was causing tiny scratches and pockmarks in the windshield of his car. Subsequently a lot of others wrote to the paper confirming that this phenomenon was widespread. Articles and letters appeared that attempted to explain this seeming anomaly. People speculated about everything from acid rain to industrial pollutants to mysterious new chemicals used to de-ice roads in winter. But consider one additional piece of information. The rash of reports of damaged windshields began only after the initial newspaper letter reporting this phenomenon. In light of this new fact, a much simpler explanation comes to mind, one that robs the whole affair of its air of mystery. As it turns out, the effect of the initial letter to the editor was to encourage people to look *at* their windshields, not *through* them. People were actually looking at their windshields closely for the first time and noticing marks and scratches that had accumulated over the years.

Many anomalies involve the sorts of extraordinary claims discussed in the last section. Often such claims derive their air of mystery from missing information, information that may suggest a plausible ordinary explanation. When confronted with such claims it is always a good idea to look for information that has been overlooked by those making the claims. Consider, for example, the strange case of crop circles. In the late 1980s, hundreds of circular and semi-circular indentations were discovered in the wheat and corn fields of southern England. There seemed to be no obvious explanation for the origin of these amazing figures. There was no evidence, for example, that people made the circles—many occurred in the middle of crop fields where there were no obvious signs of human intrusion. What was overlooked in just about every story about the circles was the fact that, near every crop circle, and in some cases even running through the circles, are what are called "tram lines." Tram lines are the indentations made by tractors as they travel through the crop fields. One of the most puzzling things about crop circles is said to be the fact that there is no sign of human intrusion. There are no footprints or bent plants leading to the circles. Thus at first glance it may seem unlikely that the circles are hoaxes. But though there are no signs of human intrusion, it is conceivable that a person could simply walk in the tram lines to the point where the circle was to be constructed yet leave no signs of intrusion. Thus, accounts of the crop circles retain much of their sense of mystery only when the facts about tram lines are ignored.[3]

You are probably familiar with some of the strange things that are said to have happened in the Bermuda Triangle, an expanse of several thousand square miles off the coast of Southern Florida. Hundreds of boats and planes have mysteriously disappeared in the area over the years. Books about the mysterious happenings in the Bermuda Triangle will typically describe in great detail cases in which it is clearly documented that a boat or plane, known to be traveling in vicinity of the Bermuda Triangle, disappeared, never to be heard from again. Yet two interesting facts are conspicuously missing in most of these reports. In many of the instances described, wreckage is subsequently found, suggesting an accident, not a mysterious disappearance. Moreover, in just about any expanse of ocean of this size near a large population area like the east coast of Florida, there will be a number of "mysterious" disappearances due to accidents, storms, inexperienced sailors and pilots, etc. Only when these facts are omitted, does the Bermuda Triangle take on the character of a great anomaly.[4]

## THE BURDEN OF PROOF

In science, as we have seen, anomalies are regarded with a healthy dose of skepticism. This attitude may at first seem at odds with the idea of an open, unbiased examination of the facts. But skepticism toward the anomalous is neither narrow-minded nor a knee-jerk defense of the status quo. A vast body of evidence is available suggesting that any given anomalous claim is probably false.

Imagine, for example, that someone were to report that they have just seen a man who was at least 10 feet tall. Now this would certainly be anomalous; it is at odds with everything we know about the limits of human growth. Of the nearly limitless number of human beings who have lived on this planet, none has come near to approaching 10 feet in height. What this means is that there is an extraordinarily large body of evidence to suggest that the claim of a 10-foot-tall man is false. Thus, lacking very strong evidence for such a claim, skepticism about its truth is only reasonable. The burden of proof, in other words, lies with the person who claims to have observed something anomalous. The more extraordinary the anomalous claim—the more extensive the evidence it is false—the more rigorous must be the evidence required before accepting the claim.

This principle—extraordinary claims require extraordinary evidence—is the basis of the skepticism with which the scientific community generally greets claims of the anomalous. It is the reason why, for example, nuclear physicists were so quickly skeptical of the claims for cold fusion. Years of accumulated experimental evidence made it a near certainty that fusion can occur only at very high temperatures and these results made perfect sense against the backdrop of the accepted theory of how atomic nuclei interact.

Though anomalous phenomena are regarded with skepticism, scientists will acknowledge the existence of such phenomena—sometimes reluctantly—when provided with unequivocal evidence. In 1986, George Bednorz and Karl Mueller of IBM's Zurich laboratory announced that they had discovered a new class of ceramic materials in which resistance-free electricity can flow at relatively high temperatures. What made this discovery something of an anomaly was the fact that superconductivity, as this phenomenon is called, was thought to be possible only at much lower temperatures. Though this discovery was startling and unexpected, the scientific community was quick to accept it once the evidence was in. Bednorz and Mueller published their results along with a detailed account of the conditions under which the material would conduct electricity with virtually no resistance at high temperatures. Other physicists were quickly able to reproduce their results. With little fanfare, a well documented anomaly was embraced by the mainstream scientific community. (Bednorz and Mueller were awarded the Nobel Prize for their discovery a year later.)

Extraordinary claims arising from sources outside of mainstream science are also at odds with a large body of contrary evidence, much of which comes from the accumulated findings of science. Here again, the burden of proof lies with advocates of such claims. Suppose a famous psychic were to claim to be able to bend keys telekinetically—by simply willing them to bend—and were to give us a demonstration. He holds an ordinary house or car key in one hand, concentrates his thoughts and the key actually seems to bend! But wait a minute. We have seen magicians perform similar feats using simple slight of hand and misdirection. Unfortunately, our psychic refuses to perform his feat in the presence of a skilled magician on the grounds that he finds it impossible to perform in the presence of people who are skeptical. Some things, claims our psychic, are not meant to be tested.

What are we to make of this demonstration? Is it a genuine feat of telekinesis or just a bit of slight of hand? The case for the latter is based on a well established scientific principle that telekinesis seems to violate. The principle is universal and has been confirmed in countless observations in every field of scientific endeavor. It is that one event cannot influence another without some intervening mechanism or medium. The flow of blood in the human body resists the pull of gravity, in part, because of the pumping action of the heart. Magnets influence the movement of metallic particles via an intervening medium, their surrounding magnetic fields. In fact there are no known instances of what is sometimes called "action at a distance"—actions or events causally related to antecedent but remote actions or events wherein there is not some intervening medium or mechanism. A variant of this principle seems to hold for human action as well. If I want to bring about a change in the world external to my mind, I must do more than "will" the change to happen. In general it is well established that a person's mind cannot effect a change in the physical world without the intervention of some physical energy or force. If, say, I want to move an object from one spot to another, simply willing the object to move is insufficient to accomplish my purposes. I must figure out some way—some sequence of actions—which will result in the goal I will myself to accomplish.

Now, it may turn out that the "no action at a distance" principle is false. It may be, that is, that we will eventually discover some phenomenon that involves action at a distance. It may even turn out that our psychic will prove to be the exception to the rule. Either that or there is some subtle medium or mechanism at work which has so far eluded our detection, another anomaly. Thus, because so much is at stake, we are entirely justified in demanding extraordinarily decisive evidence for our psychic's claim to influence objects telekinetically. In the absence of such evidence—evidence of the sort that could be provided by carefully monitored testing in the presence of a skilled magician—we have every reason to doubt our psychic's extraordinary ability. For if our psychic can do what he claims, we must take seriously the notion that forces and processes are at work in nature that have so far escaped our detection; we must begin thinking about revisions to our current understanding of things.

## SUMMARY

Observation is the first step in scientific inquiry. To ensure observational accuracy, the following criteria must be satisfied.

1. Do we have a clear sense of what the relevant phenomena are? i.e., are key terms clearly specified?

2. Can we find a way to guarantee that nothing relevant is overlooked?

3. Have we separated observational fact from conjecture or assumption?

4. Have we considered any necessary comparative information?

5. Are our observations free of expectation and belief?

Many scientific observations concern anomalies—phenomena that do not square with well established methods of explanation. Because they often pose a challenge to well documented explanations, anomalies should be regarded with a healthy dose of skepticism. What this means is that observations pertaining to an alleged anomaly should look for data that suggest that the anomaly can be explained in some conventional way. Claims about an anomalous phenomenon should be accepted only when the phenomenon has been clearly documented and shown to have no conventional explanation.

## EXERCISES

*Exercises 1–5 all involve making observations. In each case your job is to design a strategy that will allow you to make the appropriate observations. Your strategy should address both of the following. (a) Have you clarified all terms necessary to carry out your observations? (b) Have you come up with a method for checking your results, i.e., one that will minimize chances that you will miss something relevant?*

1. The number of appliances in your kitchen.

2. The length of time it takes you to fall asleep at night.

3. The amount of junk mail you receive.

4. The number of minutes devoted to news stories in a typical 30-minute television newscast.

5. The percentage of your close friends who are atheists.

*What comparative data would you need to assess the accuracy of the claims made in exercises 6–10?*

6. It seems clear that vitamin C can help prevent the common cold. Sixty percent of all people who take 200mg of vitamin C when they have a cold report that the cold runs its course within a week.

7. I can always tell when someone behind me is staring at me. Whenever I sense someone staring, I turn around just in time to catch them looking away.

8. A remarkably high number of artists and writers suffer from a serious mood disorder such as manic-depressive illness or major depression. So maybe there is something to the idea creativity and mood disorders are linked.

9. It is amazing how often the phone rings just as I am thinking about someone and it turns out to be the person I was thinking about on the other end. I guess we all have ESP to some extent.

10. SAT scores are a reliable indicator of college success. Seventy percent of those high school students who score in the top quartile and who go on to attend college complete their degree.

Semmelweis: Hungarian, germ theory of disease was unknown until he realized the effects

Four humors & bodily upucts

*Exercises 11–15 all involve actual anec-dotal reports for the extraordinary. Assess each report by answering the following questions:*

   a.   *What, if any, well established princi-ples does the report challenge?*

   b.   *Can you think of a plausible, nonextraordinary explanation for the reported event?*

   c.   *How would you rate the chances that what each passage reports is true?*

11.   Barney and Betty Hill were returning from a vacation in Canada when they reportedly saw a UFO. Then Barney inex-plicably turned their car left onto a side road. That was all the Hills remembered until two hours later, when they found themselves 35 miles farther down the road, without any idea of how they had gotten there. The Hills began to have bad dreams and finally went to see a psychiatrist, Benjamin Simon, who used hypnotic regression to bring them back to the inci-dent. Under hypnosis, the Hills said that extraterrestrials had impelled them to leave the car and walk to the spacecraft where they were separated and given examinations. Betty said alien creatures stuck a needle in her navel and took skin and nail samples. Barney claimed they took a sample of his sperm.

12.   There is a species of monkey that lives on several islands off the coast of Japan. The monkeys are often fed by humans, and in 1953 a remarkable thing was reported to have occurred. One member of the troop of mon-keys on one island learned to wash the sand off sweet potatoes she was given by dunking them in the ocean. Other members of the troop quickly picked up the habit. And then the remarkable happened. Once enough mon-keys had learned how to wash off the potatoes, suddenly all the monkeys, even on other islands hundreds of miles away, knew how to wash off the potatoes. It would seem that when the idea reached a "critical mass"—when it was known by a sufficient number of monkeys—it myste-riously spread to the species as a whole.

13.   On a few rare occasions, living human beings have mysteriously ignited and been largely con-sumed by fire. Though there are no well documented instances in which spontaneous human combustion has been witnessed, there are a number of actual cases in which the remains of a person strongly suggest sponta-neous human combustion. Typically, the body will be al-most entirely destroyed by fire, with the fire beginning in the torso and often leaving a limb or two intact. This contrasts markedly with most burning injuries, in which the limbs are likely to be the first to burn. But in cases of spontaneous human combustion, the burnt body is reduced to greasy ashes—even the bone. There is often no apparent source of flame and little damage to the victim's surroundings.

14.   In 1975, George and Kathy Lutz purchased a house in Amityville, New York. The year before, six members of the previous owner's family were murdered

in the house by another family member. Within hours of moving in, claim the Lutzes, horrible and astonishing things began to happen. Large statues moved about the house with no human assistance. Kathy Lutz levitated in her sleep. Green slime oozed from the walls. Mysterious voices were heard, sometimes saying, "Get out, get out." A large door was mysteriously ripped off its hinges. Hundreds of flies appeared seemingly from nowhere. After only twenty-eight days, the Lutzes left their new home for good.

15. In March, 1984, reporters were invited to the home of John and Joan Resch to witness the evidence of a poltergeist—a noisy and rambunctious spirit. The reporters found broken glass, dented and overturned furniture, smashed picture frames, and a household in general disarray. The focus of all this activity seemed to be the Resch's 14-year-old adopted child, Tina. The destructive activity, claimed the Resches, always occurred in close prox-

imity to Tina. Objects would mysteriously fly through the air, furniture would overturn, pictures hanging on the wall would fall to the floor, all with apparently no physical cause. Because Tina was a hyperactive and emotionally disturbed child who had been taken out of school, some parapsychologists hypothesized that the strange happenings were the result of telekinesis, not poltergeist activity.

16. *Each of the anecdotal reports in Exercises 11–15 contains an assertion about the existence of something extraordinary:*

 *a. Alien abductions.*
 *b. The instantaneous generation of ideas throughout a species.*
 *c. Spontaneous human combustion.*
 *d. Ghosts and hauntings.*
 *e. Poltergeists.*
 *f. Telekinesis.*

*Although all are quite unlikely, some seem more unlikely than others. Given what we have said about claims that challenge our current understanding of things, rate the relative likelihood of a–f, from most to least likely. Give your reasons for your ratings.*

## ANSWERS TO THE QUESTIONS ON P. 10

1. Counterclockwise.

2. Against.

3. Black, white, red, gold, and yellow.

4. Clockwise.

5. Red.

6. Right.

7. Right.

8. Right.

9. Six.

10. On the bottom.

# NOTES

1. For more on this particular puzzle, see exercises 21 and 22 on pp. 95–96.

2. As it turned out, Pons and Fleischmann were wrong for reasons that will be discussed in the next section.

3. In fact there is now evidence that many of the earliest crop circles were man-made. Several people have admitted to having made the circles and have since demonstrated to the British media how to make them in a fairly short period of time with no special equipment or tools. (See Nickell and Fischer, "The Crop Circle Phenomenon," *Skeptical Enquirer,* v. 16, no. 2, 1992.)

4. For a detailed explanation of curious events in the Bermuda Triangle, see *The Bermuda Triangle Mystery—Solved,* by Lawrence Kusche. (New York: Warner Books, 1975.)

# 3

# Proposing Explanations

## EXPLANATION

The process of proposing and then testing new explanations is at the heart of scientific method. In this chapter we will look at a number of types of explanation with which scientists deal. We will also consider how scientists respond when confronted with rival explanations for a single set of facts. Then, in Chapters 4 and 5 we will look into the way proposed explanations are put to the test. But first we need to do a bit of groundwork by clarifying just what it means to speak of a scientific explanation.

When we ask for an explanation, we could be asking for a number of things. If I'm late for an appointment with you, for example, you might ask me to explain why I'm late. Here, what you want is my excuse. Or, to take another example, you might ask your math teacher to explain how to solve a particularly nasty problem. Here you are asking to be shown how to do something. But suppose I were to bring to your attention the following rather curious fact. In many states, the letter "O" is not used on automobile license plates. You might wonder why this is the case and so you might ask me to explain. In effect, you are asking neither for an excuse nor to be taught how to do something. Instead, you are asking for the reason why something is the case, the reason many states have adopted this somewhat curious policy. (You have probably figured out the explanation for this puzzle. Most license plates are a combination of letters and numbers and the letter "O" could easily be confused with zero.) In speaking of a "scientific explanation" we are speaking of an explanation in this latter sense: an account of how or why something is the case.

Two terms often associated with explanations in science are *theory* and *hypothesis*. Both theories and hypotheses are explanatory in nature but there are some important differences between the kinds of explanations each is used to describe. "Hypothesis" may be used to refer to anything from a vague hunch to a finely detailed conjecture. In general, however, the point of characterizing a claim as an hypothesis is to note that there is something tentative and unproven about that claim. Thus, if I believe there is intelligent life in the universe somewhere other than earth, my belief may be termed an hypothesis in light of the fact I can produce no hard evidence in its favor. Proposed though untested explanations are sometimes called *explanatory hypotheses.*

"Theory" does not always imply the kind of tentativeness associated with hypotheses. A theory may be a well developed, well confirmed body of explanatory material, as in the big bang theory, the theory of evolution, or the germ theory of disease. But often people say things like, "That's only a theory," meaning roughly, "That's only your opinion of why so-and-so happened." To make matters worse, many of the things referred to in science as theories are subject to serious question. In astronomy, for example, one highly questionable alternative to the big bang theory is nonetheless referred to as the steady state theory. What typifies theories in science is the breadth and depth of their explanatory capacity. An hypothesis typically will offer an explanation for a limited range of phenomena. Theories tend to be more general structures capable of explaining a much wider variety of phenomena. Moreover, theories will often contain well confirmed rules and principles that reveal underlying explanatory similarities between apparently quite diverse phenomena. Newton's theory of motion, for example, can explain the behavior of just about anything with a mass, from the tiniest of particles to the stars and planets.

As you can see, "theory" and "hypothesis" are used to cover a lot of ground, and there is no simple and straightforward line of demarcation between the two. The net effect is that when someone speaks of a theory or an hypothesis, we may not be entirely certain what they mean. We can avoid any potential confusion in what follows by speaking simply of explanations. Explanations which share with hypotheses a kind of tentativeness, we can call *novel* or *proposed* explanations or something similar. Explanations which are well established, like some theories, we may simply characterize as *received, established, generally accepted,* etc.

New scientific explanations do not arise in an intellectual vacuum; they are occasioned by a desire to make sense of something that is not well understood—often anomalies of the sort discussed in Chapter 2. This point may seem so obvious as to hardly bear remarking. Plainly, if we understand something, there is no sense in attempting to provide it with a novel explanation. Yet two closely related points are worth keeping in mind.

First, we must resist the temptation to think of the anomalous as that which is somehow strange and unfamiliar. Now, anomalous phenomena can indeed be strange and unfamiliar, even spectacularly so. Think of some of the cases discussed in Chapter 2: crop circles, telekinesis, and the strange events of the Bermuda Triangle. Recently astronomers announced the discovery of a pair of collapsed stars that may be composed entirely of something heretofore thought impossible—free quarks. (Quarks are the building blocks of protons and neutrons and are thought to exist only in pairs and triplets.) However, much that needs explaining is considerably less mysterious and unfamiliar. The world about us is filled with phenomena with which we are more than passingly familiar, but which we do not fully understand.

We are all painfully familiar, for example, with many facts about AIDS—about how it is transmitted and what its effects are. Yet a great deal remains to be discovered about the nature of the virus and the way in which it attacks the human immune system. Perhaps nothing is more familiar in our lives than the simple fact that we are creatures capable of thought and feeling. Yet nothing is more puzzling than the way in which neurological processes in the human brain result in mental states like those involved in thought and feeling. What these examples suggest is that both the unusual and the commonplace are ripe for scientific investigation. It has often been remarked that an essential talent of a good scientific researcher is the ability to discern those mundane facts about our daily lives, the investigation of which may yield new and important insights into the ways in which our world works.

Second, the fact that you or I are puzzled by something does not mean that it is genuinely anomalous. Once again, it may seem we are remarking the obvious. Yet as we shall discover when we consider the way in which explanations are tested, it is not uncommon for a person to propose a novel explanation of something because they are unaware that somebody has already adequately explained the phenomenon in question.

The job of explaining rarely comes to an end in science. An explanation tells us something about how or why a thing happens, but rarely will an explanation be so complete as to leave no further unanswered "whys" or "hows" about the thing in question. To see this, consider the following causal explanation. We all know that the tides are caused in part by the gravitational attraction of the moon. Thus, we can explain the tides by reference to the fact that there is a large amount of water on the surface of the earth, that the earth rotates on its axis, and that the source of gravitational attraction, the moon, moves in orbit around the earth. Now, though our explanation clearly gives us a sense of why there should be two high and low tides roughly every twenty-four hours, it leaves a lot unexplained. What is the process by which gravitating bodies, in this case the moon and the oceans, interact? Put another way, how is it that massive objects such as these have an effect on one another? We might cite here something called the law of gravity: objects tend to attract one another in direct proportion to their masses and in inverse proportion to the square of the distance between them. In a sense, this adds a bit of detail to our explanation. But why should this "law" hold? Why should objects attract one another at all, let alone in just this regular, law-like fashion? Unfortunately, we must leave these questions unanswered, for little is yet known about what physicists today call the "carrier" of gravitational interaction, "the graviton."

As our last example suggests, explaining one thing in science often leads naturally to the need for new, more fundamental explanations. The moral of this last point is that in science, at any rate, progress is largely a matter of providing better and better approximations of what is going on in nature. Rarely are explanations final or complete in the sense of leaving no additional unanswered questions about what is really going on.

Scientific progress is not always a matter of supplementing received explanations with more subtle but complementary new explanations. The history of science is fraught with instances in which received explanations have been supplanted by novel and radically different ones. One of the most well known examples of the replacement of one explanation with another is the gradual shift from the Ptolemaic conception of the universe to the Copernican.

In the Ptolemaic view, systematized about 140 A.D. by Ptolemy Claudius of Alexandria, the stationary earth stands at the center of the universe and all heavenly objects revolve around the earth. The Ptolemaic view had considerable explanatory power in that by a series of complicated calculations, the motions of all celestial objects known at the time—the sun, the moon, the five innermost planets, and the stars—could be explained, though in ways very different than we would explain them today. For example, careful observation revealed that Mars generally moves eastward across the night sky but occasionally appears to move backward for a bit before resuming its eastward course. In the Ptolemaic view, all celestial objects trace out circular orbits around the earth. Ptolemy explained the backwards, or retrograde, motion of Mars by introducing the notion of an epicycle—a small circular loop in the orbit of Mars such that, from an earthly perspective, Mars would actually appear to stop and then move backwards during its epicycle. A tribute to its explanatory value is the fact that the Ptolemaic view dominated Western thought for more than a thousand years.

In the sixteenth century, however, Nicholas Copernicus, a Polish scientist and astronomer, proposed a new and radically different view of the cosmos. In Copernicus's view, many of the basic assumptions of Ptolemy were wrong. The sun, not the earth, is at the center of things; two of the planets, Mercury and Venus, occupy orbits nearer the sun than does the earth; and, what is more, many celestial motions are to be explained by the fact that the earth rotates on its axis. One advantage of the Copernican view is that it suggests a very different explanation for retrograde motion than does that of Ptolemy. If, as Copernicus suggested, the orbit of Mars is outside that of the earth, then the double motion of Mars with respect to the earth explains the apparent backward motion of Mars. For in Copernicus's view, we observe the motion of Mars from a location that is itself moving through space with the net effect that Mars will on occasion appear to be moving backwards.

There are a number of interesting facts about this particular episode in the history of science. The first, of course, is the enormous shift in thinking about the nature of celestial motions occasioned by the work of Copernicus. One might think the Copernican "revolution," as it is sometimes called, would have ushered in a new level of accuracy and simplicity in the calculation of planetary motions. But as it turned out, Copernicus's explanation was neither more accurate nor even much simpler than that of Ptolemy. Both views explained roughly the same collection of data about planetary motion. Moreover, like Ptolemy, Copernicus had to introduce a number of epicycles into his work to make his explanation fit the facts. The real value, then, of Copernicus's achievement resides in the simple but profoundly new way of thinking about celestial motion it introduced.

But our story does not end here. Though in rough outline the Copernican view of the universe finally replaced that of Ptolemy, many of the details of the Copernican view were themselves eventually rejected. Copernicus, like Ptolemy, for example, believed that the planets trace out circular orbits around the sun. (In fact, it was this conviction that necessitated the introduction of the occasional epicycle in his calculations.) It remained for Johannes Kepler, nearly a century later, to discover that the planets trace out elliptical orbits around the sun. Kepler thereby reduced the kinds of motion required to explain the observed positions of the planets and did away, finally, with the infamous epicycle. In defense of Copernicus, it must be noted that Kepler had available much more accurate measurements of the movement of the planets than anything available to either Copernicus or Ptolemy. Yet despite the enormous import of Kepler's contributions to our understanding of celestial motion, it remained for astronomers long after the time of Kepler to refine the Copernican world view even further by removing the sun from its exalted position at the center of the universe.

## CAUSES

When we think about what is involved in giving an explanation, the notions of cause and effect come immediately to mind. Indeed, the most obvious kind of explanation is causal explanation. Why, for example, when we were small children, did teeth, carefully tucked under our pillows, vanish only to be replaced by money? Because while we were sleeping our parents removed the teeth and replaced them with money. Why is there a circular crater several miles in diameter in the Arizona desert? Because a large meteor survived intact its trip through the earth's atmosphere; its crash produced the crater. Why is smoking on the increase among young adults? In part, because the tobacco industry targets this segment of the population in much of its advertising. In each of these cases a cause for a particular effect is identified and with each we understand something of why the phenomena in question is the case.

Causal explanations are common in our daily lives. Imagine I've arrived late for a lunch engagement. "Sorry I'm late. The traffic was horrendous," I say. What I am doing here is claiming that something out of my control caused me to be late. Or suppose the street out front of the restaurant where we are meeting is flooded. You venture the guess that all of the drains are clogged with leaves. Your guess involves a causal explanation. The leaves covering the drains have caused the street to flood.

Causal relationships are not always as simple or straightforward as our last example. For one thing, effects can have more than a single cause. It may be, for example, that my lateness was in part caused by a traffic jam. But suppose that while hung up in traffic I ran low on gas and so had to stop and fill up. Suppose also that neither event alone would have made me late. In the jargon of causal research, multiple related causes are referred to simply as "causal factors." Moreover, effects need not invariably be associated with a given causal factor. We know, for example, that cigarette smoking causes lung cancer despite the fact that some cigarette smokers will not contract lung cancer and that some who will contract lung cancer will not be smokers. As this last example suggests, causal explanations are often about groups, not individuals. The claim that smoking causes lung cancer means that, among people in general (and several kinds of laboratory animals), smoking is one factor that contributes to lung cancer. Finally, causes can be either *remote* or *proximate*. If, say, A causes B, which in turn causes C, A is often referred to as a proximate cause of B and a remote cause of C. So, for example, if I trip and bump into the table where you are seated causing your water glass to spill in your lap, my tripping is a proximate cause of the movement of the table and a remote cause of the mess in your lap.

## CORRELATION

Closely related to the notion of a causal explanation is that of a correlation. Indeed, people often assume that if two things are correlated they are causally linked. But this assumption is often wrong. A correlation is nothing more than a comparison between a pair of characteristics within a population. Those characteristics are correlated if they display some regular, measurable variance. The simplest sort of correlation involves the comparison of two groups, one having a given characteristic and the other lacking it. If a second characteristic occurs at different frequencies in the two groups, it is correlated with one of the two. Suppose, for example, that we compared two groups of people, all between ages 30 and 49. Each member of the first group has completed at least four years of college, while those in the second group have completed less than four. Suppose also that we were able to look at the average annual income of the two groups and were to find that the income of the first group is, on average, 20 percent higher than that of the second group. This means there is a correlation between education and income in the groups of people we have considered.

Correlations can be positive or negative. If a characteristic occurs at a greater frequency in one group than in the other, it is positively correlated with the first group; if it occurs at a lesser frequency, the correlation is negative. By contrast, if the characteristic occurs at roughly the same frequency in both groups, there is no correlation between the characteristic and either group. In our example, we have uncovered a positive correlation between education and income. Suppose instead we had found that the income of those having four or more years of college was actually lower than that of people with less education. This finding would suggest a negative correlation between the two factors. Had we found no real difference in levels of income, we would have to conclude that, insofar as we can tell, there is no correlation between level of education and income. (This does not mean there is no such correlation. All we can conclude is that our quick check of the data available shows no correlation!)

Correlations can also hold between pairs of characteristics within a single group. Within a group, if two measurable characteristics vary in a somewhat regular and predictable fashion, they are correlated. Suppose, for example, we had at our disposal a large amount of information about the freshman class at a small local college. Examining the data we find what appears to be an interesting relationship between first semester grade point averages (GPA) and scholastic aptitude test (SAT) scores. About 100 students completed the first semester. In most cases, say 75 or so, we find that GPA varies directly with SAT score. That is, if we arrange these 75 students in order of ascending SAT score, we find a corresponding increase in GPAs; the higher the SAT score, the higher the GPA. For the other 25 or so students, we find no regular variance. Some students with relatively high SAT scores have relatively low GPAs and vice versa. Some with average SAT scores have relatively high, some relatively low GPAs. Despite these exceptions, our findings suggest a positive correlation between SAT score and GPA, at least in the group we have examined. Had we found just the reverse—had we found that for most students, GPA diminished when SAT scores increased, we would have uncovered a negative correlation between SAT score and GPA. Suppose instead we were to discover no regular variance between SAT scores and GPAs; many students with relatively high SAT scores had average or low GPAs while many with relatively low SAT scores had average or high GPAs. This would suggest that no correlation exits between SAT score and GPA in the freshman class of the college.

As our last example suggests, correlation is seldom an all or nothing matter. A perfect correlation between two characteristics would require a one-to-one correspondence between changes in the two. (In our example, increases in SAT score would need to be accompanied by increases in GPA in all 100 cases to establish a perfect correlation.) But particularly when groups of subjects are large, the fact that a correlation is somewhat less than perfect does not undercut its potential significance, perhaps as a predictor of one characteristic in cases where we know something about the quantity of the other. Presuming, in our example, that we have uncovered a fairly consistent positive correlation between SAT score and first semester GPA, we may be able to predict something about a new college student's chances of success based on his or her SAT score. But here we need to introduce a crucial note of caution. Any inference we draw about an individual, based on the evidence of a correlation, assumes a causal connection between the correlated characteristics. And this assumption is not always warranted. The fact that two things are correlated does not, by itself, indicate that the two are causally linked.

Why this is so can be seen in the following examples. If we were to examine a group of similar people, say, members of a single trade or profession, we could probably unearth a number of correlations. We might find, for example, a correlation between age and income. (Established either by showing a regular variance between age and income for the whole group or by showing that people above and below a certain age have, on average, different income levels.) We would probably also find a correlation between age and the use of reading glasses. Given these correlations, it is likely we will also find a correlation between income and the use of reading glasses! Now, none of these correlations seems to be a coincidence. There seems to be a clear link between age and the need for reading glasses. But the link in the other two cases is much more tenuous. Advancing age does not cause one's income level to rise nor does income have any bearing on the need for reading glasses. The link in these two cases is undoubtedly explained by some other factor or series of factors. For example, in most trades or professions the longer one works at a job, the more one generally makes. This, then, accounts for the correlation between age and income.

To make matters worse, a correlation may be evidence of nothing more than coincidence, a "mere correlation." This is because unrelated things can vary in regular, measurable ways. For a number of years now, two things have regularly increased: the sale of Burger King Whoppers and the number of minutes per day of television watched by children. Come to think of it, recent increases in Whopper sales are correlated, negatively, with a gradual but regular decrease, in the same period, in the number of people who go bowling! And since we are an aging population, I suspect we could also dredge up a correlation between Whopper sales and the purchase of reading glasses. These new correlations, of course, suggest nothing more than that lots of things, many of them not causally related, vary over time in somewhat regular ways.

All of this is not to say the search for correlations is not an important component of causal research. Indeed, if two things are causally linked, they will be correlated, and so evidence of a correlation may provide some initial evidence for a causal link. But the simple fact that two things are correlated is, by itself, not evidence of a causal link. In Chapter 5 we will look closely at the ways in which claims about causal links and their attendant correlations are tested. For now, it is enough to keep in mind that correlations do not necessarily indicate causal links and, for this reason, are of less explanatory value than are facts about causal links.

Explanations in science do not always involve the attribution of causes to effects. Why do our eyelids blink open and shut several times every minute? To keep the surface of the eyes moist. Why does a gun kick as it is discharged? Because of a well known physical law: for every action there is an equal and opposite reaction. Neither of these explanations involves a cause, at least in any straightforward sense. Causes are events occurring before their effects. The law of motion we have just invoked is not a discrete event. The goal accomplished by the blinking of the eyes is not antecedent to the event it is introduced to explain. As we will find next, scientific explanations can take many forms. They can involve general laws and can turn on the function a thing plays in some larger enterprise, techniques illustrated in the cases above. They can also involve underlying processes and causal mechanisms, techniques often used to enrich strong correlation ≠ no cause + effect

## QUICK REVIEW 3.1    Causation and Correlation

### Causation

Two things are causally linked if one proceeds and is responsible for the other. Suppose your car won't start because its battery is dead. The dead battery is the cause and your car's failure to start, the effect. Effects can have more than a single cause and there may be many causes for similar effects. Several causal factors are responsible for the behavior of the stock market and a market decline can be caused by a variety of factors. Causal relationships can hold between individual events or between large classes of events as in the claim that megadoses of vitamin C can reduce occurrences of the common cold. If events are causally linked, they will be correlated, but correlations do not necessarily indicate causal links.

### Positive Correlation

In two populations, P and Q are positively correlated if a greater percentage of Ps than non-Ps have Q. Suppose that nationwide, people with cell phones have, on average, a higher income than people wihout cell phones. Cell-phone ownership and income are positively correlated. In a single population, if a regular increase in one trait, P, is accompanied by a regular increase in another, Q, then the two are positively correlated. Suppose worker productivity at a plant increases as pay increases though with some exceptions. Worker productivity is positively correlated with income.

### Negative Correlation

In the two populations, P and Q are negatively correlated if a smaller percentage of P's than non-P's have Q. Suppose regular users of the local public library (once or more a month) watch, on average, much less TV than sporadic or nonusers of the library. TV watching and library use are negatively correlated for the group in question. In a single population, P and Q are negatively correlated if a regular increase in P is accompanied by a regular decrease in Q. Suppose that the number of visits to the library per month increases as the average number of hours watching TV decreases. Library use and TV watching are negatively correlated.

### No Correlation

In two populations, P and Q are not correlated if there is no difference in levels of Q in P and not-P. If equal percentages of males and females are left-handed, there is no correlation between left-handedness and gender. In a single population two traits are not correlated if there is no regular variance between the occurrence of the two. Suppose we were to record both the number of checks written and the number of soft drinks consumed per month by a randomly chosen group of people. We would probably find no evidence that variation in one trait is a predictor of a variation in the other. This suggests there is no correlation between the two.

### Perfect Correlation

An invariant relation between two traits; for every change in one trait there is a consistent change in the other. In most species of trees, age in years is perfectly correlated with the number of rings in the tree's trunk; the older the tree the greater the number of rings, without exception.

simple causal explanations. Let's now take a closer look at each of these four types of explanation.

## CAUSAL MECHANISMS

We can know that one thing is the cause of another without fully understanding what is responsible for the link. We know, for example, that smoking causes lung cancer. Yet despite the fact that we are quite confident there is a link between smoking and lung cancer, little is known about the mechanism—the physiological process—by which the carcinogens ("carcinogen" just means "cancer causing agent") in cigarette smoke lead to uncontrolled cell growth in the lungs of the smoker. In science, explanations often involve claims about causal mechanisms: the processes intervening between a remote cause and its effect.

A recent study revealed an apparent causal connection between aspirin consumption and the risk of heart attack. According to the study, men who take a single buffered aspirin every other day have a 50 percent lower chance of having a heart attack than do men who do not take aspirin. Here the connection between aspirin consumption and risk of heart attack seems to be fairly well documented. As it turns out, the causal mechanism by which aspirin reduces the risk of heart attack is also well understood. Aspirin interferes with the first stage of the blood's clotting process. Now, many heart attacks are caused by blood clots in damaged arteries. It seems that when the thin inner wall of an artery is damaged, aspirin inhibits the tendency of minute blood platelets to clot over the damaged area. Thus, aspirin reduces the clotting effect that can lead to serious heart attack.

To take a very different example, one more closely related to the use of explanation by causal mechanism in our daily lives, imagine the following.[1] A friend applied for a job she really wanted to get. Yet now she tells us she finds the job utterly uninteresting and probably wouldn't accept it even if it were offered to her. Why the change in attitude? We discover subsequently that our friend learned she had no chance of getting the job. But how, if at all, did this bring about her change in attitude about the job? The answer may well lie in a causal mechanism, often called cognitive dissonance reduction, that makes people cease desiring that which they cannot get; you may be familiar with this mechanism under its more common name, sour grapes. Having learned she wouldn't get the job, our friend adjusted her desires to reduce the dissonance caused by wanting something she could not have. No doubt the notion of cognitive dissonance reduction is a bit less precise than is the mechanism invoked to explain the connection between aspirin and heart disease, and for that reason would be more difficult to test. But such psychological mechanisms nonetheless play an important role in our attempts at explaining why people behave as they do.

# UNDERLYING PROCESSES

In 1828 the Scottish botanist, Robert Brown, discovered that when tiny particles are suspended in a liquid they undergo a constant quivering motion. This phenomenon—called Brownian motion—remained a mystery until it was explained in a 1905 paper by Albert Einstein. Brownian motion is due to the constant buffeting of the suspended particles by the ever moving molecules of the liquid. In this explanation, the movement of the particles in the liquid is redescribed in terms of the properties of the liquid's component parts. Underlying processes, unlike causal mechanisms, do not attempt to "fill in the gap" between cause and effect by positing intervening causes. Rather the point is to redescribe the phenomenon, only now at a more basic level. Molecular bombardment is thus not the cause of Brownian motion. Molecular bombardment *is* Brownian motion described from the point of view of molecular chemistry, a point of view that sheds considerable explanatory insight into the nature of the phenomenon.

Explanation by underlying processes is sometimes said to be reductionistic, in that descriptions of phenomena at one level are reduced to descriptions at another, more basic level. Reductive descriptions can be technical and usually will make use of explanatory notions that do not occur in the original description. You may, for example, be aware that fluorescent lamps are much more efficient than traditional incandescent bulbs. The explanation lies in the way each produces light. When light is produced by incandescent bulbs, the following process takes place. Electrical energy passes through a wire, heating it until it incandesces (glows). The wire, called a filament, typically is made of a metal called tungsten; the enclosing bulb around the filament directs or diffuses the light. The problem is that 90 percent of the energy put into such a bulb is released in the form of heat while only 10 percent results in light. Fluorescent lamps produce light in a different way, by energizing gas. Electrical energy flows into electrodes at the ends of a tube. The electrodes emit electrons, which energize a small amount of mercury vapor held at very low temperatures inside the tube. The energized mercury molecules radiate ultraviolet light, which is in turn absorbed by a phosphorescent coating on the inside of the surface of the tube, thus producing visible light. This process produces very little heat; fluorescent lamps are able to convert almost 90 percent of the energy they consume into light. So, the amount of electrical energy required by a fluorescent lamp to produce a given amount of light is substantially less than that required by incandescent bulbs. In redescribing incandescence and fluorescence in terms of the behavior of their underlying constituents, we have introduced a host of new explanatory notions: electrons, electrodes, filaments, and gasses, and the way in which electrons behave under various conditions. In effect, we have explained the greater efficiency of fluorescence over incandescence by looking carefully at what is going on at a more fundamental level in each process.

## LAWS

What happens if heat is applied to a closed container of a gas? Pressure increases. Why? An important law governing the behavior of gasses, discovered by Joseph Gay-Lussac, provides the answer to our question. Gay-Lussac's law tells us: if volume is held constant, the pressure exerted by a gas will vary directly with the temperature. So, as we increase the temperature of a gas by applying heat, we increase the pressure in the closed container. Such laws explain by revealing how particular events are instances of more general regularities in nature.

A law is universal when it claims that a particular kind of behavior will occur in all (or in no) cases. Thus, Gay-Lussac's Law is universal in that it makes a claim about the behavior of all gasses. But scientific laws need not be universal; some laws claim only that a particular kind of behavior will occur in a certain proportion of cases.

Suppose we were to learn that a good friend, a nurse, has contracted hepatitis B. We are aware that he works in a clinical setting where patients with hepatitis B are regularly treated. We are also aware that recent studies have shown an alarmingly high number of health care workers contract the hepatitis virus from their clients—one out of four health care workers who are accidentally exposed to the virus will actually contract hepatitis B.[2] It seems a real possibility that our friend's condition is explained, in part, by the statistic we have just cited. The explanation we might give would go something like the following:

> Exposed health care workers have a 25 percent chance of contracting hepatitis B. Friend F is a nurse who works in a setting where the risk of exposure to hepatitis B is high. F has hepatitis B. Thus, it is likely F has contracted hepatitis B from a client.

Though this explanation involves a law, it is not universal; it does not claim that everyone who is exposed to hepatitis B will contract it. Here we have an example of explanation by law, but where the law on which we rely claims only that a certain proportion of those exposed will contract hepatitis B.

No doubt it seems odd to call this claim a "law," yet it is certainly law-like, in just the way Gay-Lussac's law is law-like. Both describe regular correspondences. In the case of Gay-Lussac's law, the correspondence is between the pressure, volume, and temperature of a gas, while in the case of our latter law, the correspondence is between workers who are exposed to the virus and workers who subsequently contract hepatitis B. The difference is that laws of the latter sort, what are often called *statistical laws,* enable us to give explanations that must be carefully qualified. It may be that our friend has contracted the hepatitis virus from someone or something other than a client and, as our statistical law tells us, chances are quite good that exposure to clients with the virus will not lead to infection. Thus, we have to qualify our explanation by adding the phrase, "it is likely," to acknowledge the possibility that our explanation may be wrong for this particular case.

Statistical laws often stand behind simple causal explanations of the sort discussed earlier. Consider again one of our examples. I claimed that I was late for a luncheon date because of a traffic jam. I suspect you would accept this excuse in part because you are aware that generally, when people are stuck in traffic, their travel time is increased. Interestingly enough, if you did not believe this statistical law you would probably not buy my excuse.

## FUNCTION

We often explain the things we and others do (and don't do) by reference to our hopes, wants, aspirations, beliefs, etc. "Why," I might ask, "are you only having a salad for lunch?" "Because," you might explain, "I want to lose a few pounds." To explain one thing by reference to the purpose it fulfills is to give a functional explanation. And so, to explain our behavior by reference to what we hope to achieve, as in the example above, is to give one sort of functional explanation. Human behavior is not the only thing susceptible to explanation by reference to function or purpose. If you asked me about the rock sitting on my desk, I would offer the following explanation. A heating duct is located just over my desk, and whenever the heat comes on, unsecured papers blow about. So I use the rock as a paperweight. Following a similar strategy, we might explain that a carburetor is the component of an internal combustion engine that mixes fuel and oxygen. In both of these examples, we explain by specifying the purpose the thing in question serves. The purpose of the rock on my desk is to hold down papers; the purpose of a carburetor is to mix fuel and oxygen.

In the social sciences, functional explanation plays a central role. An historian or economist, for example, might explain the emergence of a social practice—say, slavery or liberalized abortion laws—by reference to the role such practices play in some larger social or economic enterprise. Slavery, it seems, was instrumental in the development of economies of scale in eighteenth century United States. Liberalized abortion laws adopted in the 1960s reflected changing attitudes about the role of women in society, and thus provided women greater latitude in making decisions about their future.

As the examples above suggest, functional explanations often make reference to the purpose or purposes of that which is being explained. Because of this, it may seem that functional explanation will be useful in dealing only with human contrivances and behavior. But functional explanations can provide insight into other sorts of cases as well, cases in which "purpose" implies nothing about human intervention, planning, or forethought. For example, functional explanations are often used in the biological sciences. One of the most influential figures in the scientific revolution was the British physician, William Harvey (1578–1657). Perhaps Harvey's greatest accomplishment was his discovery that the purpose of the heart is to act as a sort of pump, facilitating the circulation of the blood. Similarly, evolutionary biologists often explain the

---

**QUICK REVIEW 3.2**   Ways of Explaining

---

**Causes**

To explain one thing or event by reference to another, antecedent thing or event. *Examples:* "Debris from last night's windstorm caused the power outage." "Excessive alcohol consumption can damage the liver."

**Causal Mechanisms**

To explain by citing intervening causal factors, factors that explain the effects of a more distant cause. *Examples:* "Debris from the storm severed several power lines thus causing last night's power outage."

**Laws**

To explain an event by referring to a general law or principle of which the event is an instance. *Example:* "The fuel efficiency of a vehicle is determined in part by size and weight. This is because acceleration is directly proportional to force but inversely proportional to mass. Thus, the larger the object you want to move, the greater the force you need

to apply, and so the more energy you need to expend."

**Underlying Processes**

To explain something by reference to the working of its component parts. *Example:* "The chest pain and breathing difficulty symptomatic of pneumonia results from an infection of the lung tissue. The tiny air sacs of which the lungs are composed—called alveoli—fill with inflammatory fluid caused by the infection. As a result, the flow of oxygen through the alveolar walls is greatly impaired."

**Function**

To explain something by reference to the role it fulfills in some larger enterprise. *Examples:* "Many species of birds build their nests in high places—trees, cliffs, etc.—to protect their young from predators." "The lungs serve as a means of both introducing oxygen into and removing carbon dioxide from the blood stream."

---

dominance of a trait within a species on the basis of the advantage it confers on those that have the trait—on, that is, the purpose it serves.

But in such cases, "purpose" need not be understood on the model of human purposes. Rather, "purpose," as it is used in biological explanations, means something more like "role in some larger enterprise." To give the purpose is to specify that role. So, for example, to wonder about the purpose served by the bright colors of many species of flowers is merely to consider how this trait is beneficial in the propagation of those species. Bees, it seems, are attracted to brightly colored flowers and thus bright coloration tends to enhance the chances of pollination. In a perfectly harmless sense then, the "purpose" of a bright coloration in some flower species is to attract potential pollinators. But in this sense, to explain by reference to the purpose served by a trait is not to suggest anything like the underlying intelligence we associate with human purposes.

# THE INTERDEPENDENCE
# OF EXPLANATORY METHODS

Earlier we noted that in science the need for explanation rarely comes to an end. This fact is reflected in the interdependence of the various types of explanation we have just considered. Put simply, more than one type of explanatory claim may be involved in a chain of explanations. Knowing, for example, that the function of a carburetor is to mix fuel and oxygen, we might then go on to consider how a carburetor accomplishes this goal. And here we will probably need something like a causal mechanism. We will, in other words, need to consider how a carburetor's parts operate in conjunction with one another to accomplish the proper mixture of fuel and oxygen. To go even deeper, we may want to consider underlying processes by thinking about the chemical reactions that contribute to combustion. A sense of the function something performs, thus, can often guide our understanding of how and why it works as it does. (This strategy is sometimes called "reverse engineering." First figure out what a thing is intended to do. Then consider how it is designed and built to accomplish that end.)

Or, to take another kind of case, if we want to understand more about a particular causal connection, we will need to speculate about causal mechanisms that may be involved. A lake is polluted and some of its indigenous species of wildlife begin to diminish. There seems to be a connection. But what is the process by which greater pollution leads to less and less wildlife? Similarly, if we want to understand more about why a law-like regularity obtains, we may need to consider underlying processes. Recall our discussion earlier of Gay-Lussac's Law: if volume is held constant, the pressure exerted by a gas will vary directly with the temperature. Why, we might wonder, should this particular relationship between temperature, volume, and pressure hold for gasses? The answer to this question requires that we examine the processes underlying the phenomenon described by our gas law. In fact, gasses are composed of molecules rushing hither and thither at enormous speeds. Pressure on the container holding the gas is a result of gas molecules colliding with the walls of the container. When heat is applied to the container, it is translated into increased activity on the part of the molecules of gas. The result is that the number of collisions with the container increases, thereby increasing the pressure exerted on the container by the gas. (This is a very rough sketch of a basic notion in what is called the kinetic theory of gasses.)

Or if we want to understand more about a process underlying something we may need to look once again for causal mechanisms and law-like regularities, considerably more fine grained in character. To return for a moment to our story about the process involved in fluorescent lighting, why would mercury molecules, bombarded by electrons, radiate ultraviolet light? To answer this question we would need to consider processes that intervene and perhaps even underlie the interaction of electrons and mercury molecules.

You may well wonder whether the process of explaining can ever come to an end, and, if so, where this end might be. These are deep and profoundly difficult philosophical issues. Some philosophers believe that as a given science matures, claims about causal connections and mechanisms will be replaced gradually by broader and broader laws describing more and more causal phenomena. On this view, the most fundamental kind of scientific understanding is that provided when laws are discovered that reveal something about the interconnectedness of a wide variety of phenomena; the wider the variety, the greater the understanding. Other philosophers would maintain that at least in certain sorts of cases, perhaps all, to explain a thing is to identify its immediate cause or causes and that when we can find no further intervening mechanism, the process of explanation must come to an end. In this view, law-like statements, no matter how broad and unifying, merely help us to classify and describe the rather more basic causal process at work in nature. For our purposes, however, we need not wrestle with these deep philosophical issues. Suffice it to say, the kind of explanatory claim one will give—whether it be about causes, causal mechanisms, laws, underlying process, or something else—will depend on how much one knows and, of course, what it is one wants to explain.

## RIVAL EXPLANATIONS
## AND OCKHAM'S RAZOR

Often it may be possible to conceive of more than one explanation for something that is not well understood. Many of the examples discussed in Chapter 2 involved rival explanations. Are crop circles messages from alien beings? Are they hoaxes? Is cold fusion the result of a chemical or a nuclear reaction? Do people actually leave their bodies during near death experiences? Are they suffering from something like a hallucination brought on by the stressful conditions they are under? The first step in sorting through rival explanations is to apply a simple principle, Ockham's Razor or, as it is sometimes called, the principle of parsimony. To see what this principle involves, consider the following case. Imagine that you are unable to find your keys. You have searched all morning to no avail and you know they should be around the house somewhere because you remember using them to open the door when you came home late last night. One possible explanation is that you've simply put them somewhere that you haven't looked yet. But other explanations are available as well. Perhaps someone who shares the house with you has inadvertently taken your keys instead of theirs. These two explanations rival one another in that either, if true, would serve to explain the phenomenon in question. Presumably, at least one of the two is wrong, though in just the right circumstances I suppose they might both be correct.

What makes one explanation more plausible than its rivals is a bit more difficult to say. Let's begin by considering a couple of explanations for your missing keys that are a bit more bizarre than the two we have considered so far. Perhaps someone broke into your house while you were asleep and stole them. Or perhaps they just disappeared into thin air. Compare these two new explanations with the first explanation we proposed above—that you have simply misplaced your keys. Our first explanation is at least fairly plausible in that it makes no reference to other things which themselves stand in need of explanation. Surely, you've misplaced things before, only to have them turn up even after you were convinced they were lost forever.

Consider, next, the first of our rather more bizarre explanations: somebody stole your keys. Keep in mind here, the point of an explanation is to make sense of how or why something has happened. If in giving an explanation we invoke things which are themselves quite puzzling, we have really only avoided the question of why the thing in question happened. Why would someone break into your house and only take your keys? And why is there no evidence of forced entry? Though I suppose these things could be explained—maybe we are dealing with an incredibly clever and skilled burglar who intends to return when you are not home—I think you can see that each additional explanation makes the original explanation seem less and less likely. Now, a whole string of events would have to occur in order for our second explanation to retain some sense of plausibility. Our final explanation does no good at all. The keys have just "disappeared into thin air?" How does this work? Were they consumed by a tiny black hole? Did they spontaneously melt? In the name of resolving a simple puzzle, our final explanation has embraced ideas that are radically anomalous and, judging by what we know of nature, false.

Our two bizarre explanations violate *Ockham's Razor.*[3] This principle is named after its author, a Medieval philosopher and monk, William of Ockham (1285–1349). Ockham's own version of the Razor is somewhat obscure: "What can be done with fewer is done in vain with more." A more appropriate version of this principle for our purposes is the following: given competing explanations, any of which would, if true, explain a given puzzle, we should initially opt for the explanation which itself contains the least number of puzzling notions. The rationale behind this admonition should be clear. If a puzzle can be explained without introducing any additional puzzling notions, there is no good reason to entertain any explanation that involves additional puzzles.

By comparison with our two bizarre explanations, our first explanation— that you have put your keys somewhere you haven't looked yet—fits the bill here. So, to say that one of a series of rival explanations is the most plausible is to say it is the one most in keeping with Ockham's Razor. Keep in mind that Ockham's Razor does not rule out explanations which themselves involve notions not fully understood. Rather it only suggests that given competing explanations, we should favor the one which involves the least number of problematic notions. Forced to choose between clever burglars and black holes to account for the missing keys, Ockham's Razor would suggest the former.

## EXPLANATION AND DESCRIPTION

In this and the last chapter we have discussed two key elements of scientific method: observation and explanation. Unfortunately, many reports of extraordinary happenings of the sort discussed in Chapter 2 blur the distinction between these two key notions. Ideally, observations should be couched in purely descriptive language, language that tells us what occurred—no more, no less. But often reports of extraordinary events contain a good deal that is not purely descriptive. Imagine, for example, someone were to report awakening in the middle of the night to discover what appeared to be their long-departed grandmother standing at the foot of the bed. They might subsequently claim:

(1) I saw the ghost of my dead grandmother.

But what, precisely, is factual in (1)? What, that is, can we be confident actually happened? That the person had an extraordinary experience is clear. Beyond this it is hard to know just what to say. Consider two rival accounts of what may have happened:

(2) X had a vivid life-like dream in which X's grandmother appeared.

(3) Somebody played an elaborate but vicious prank on X in the middle of the night.

(1) through (3) implicitly contain explanations of the event in question. That is to say, each presupposes the truth of a very different explanation: (1) that what the person actually saw was a ghost; (2) that what he or she "saw" was part of a dream; and (3) that what was seen was real, but a hoax, not a ghost.

Similarly, many anecdotal reports of the extraordinary contain much more than a simple, objective description of the experience. Such reports often blend fact with untested explanation and are what we might call *explanation laden*. For example, "The flying saucer hovered over the horizon and then accelerated away at a fantastic rate," tells us a couple of things about a person who might claim to have witnessed such an event. First, the person had an undeniably extraordinary experience. Second, the person believes the proper explanation for the experience is that he or she actually saw an intelligently controlled spacecraft.

In evaluating such a report, we must do our best to separate the descriptive wheat from the explanatory chaff. If we are able to subtract out the explanation laden portions of a report of the extraordinary, we may be able to arrive at a clear sense of what actually was experienced and, thus, what needs to be explained. Think once again of our flying saucer report. Suppose we could establish, for example, that the person making the report actually saw a bright light near the horizon, looked away to call to a friend, looked again and saw only a dim, twinkling light at some distance from the original light. Having gotten clear on this much, we would at least be in a position to think about rival explanations more plausible that the one implicit in the initial description of the event.

I once spoke with a person who claimed to have lived in a haunted house. He recalled that every few nights he would hear a knocking at the front door despite the fact that there was never anyone there when he opened it. We agreed that a more accurate description of the experience would contain only the salient facts: on several occasion he heard a series of sounds, very much like knocking at the door, and the sounds seemed to come from the area of the house near the front door. He also added that he was never near the door when he heard the noise. Once we focused on this new, more objective description, several plausible explanations immediately came to mind; a tree or bush knocking against the house or perhaps some activity outside or even inside that sounded, from a distance, like knocking. Now, we may never discover what really happened on those nights when the person in this episode heard a " knocking" at the door. At the very least, however, we know what parts of the story are fact, what parts speculation. And this is the real value of carefully distinguishing between the descriptive and explanatory elements of an extraordinary claim.

## SUMMARY

An explanation, in science, is an account of how or why something has come to be the case. Both theories and hypotheses involve explanations. Theories tend to be broad, unifying explanations while hypotheses are more limited in scope. Both can be tentative or well confirmed. Scientific explanations can make reference to causes, causal mechanisms, underlying processes, laws or function, all of which are summarized in the Quick Review on p. 39. Explanations often leave some explanatory questions about the phenomenon in question unanswered. To enrich an explanation of one type, other types of explanation may need to be given. Correlations alone explain very little unless they are accompanied by evidence that the correlated terms are either directly or indirectly linked.

Competing explanations for a single set of facts can be evaluated by the use of Ockham's Razor—a principle to the effect that among rival explanations, the one containing the least number of puzzling notions is most likely to be true. Many apparently descriptive claims contain explanatory elements. In such cases, it will be necessary to isolate the descriptive elements in order to begin thinking about possible explanations.

## EXERCISES

*Exercises 1–15 involve explanations of one sort or other. For each exercise, answer the following questions:*

1. *What is being explained?*
2. *What is the explanation?*
3. *What, if any, recognizable sorts of explanatory claims occur in the explanation?*

*Your choices are: causes, causal mechanisms, laws, underlying processes, or function. Some of the exercises may involve more than one sort of explanation.*
*(Note: On page 50 a solution is provided for Exercise 1.)*

1. The spinal column is composed of bones (vertebrae) that are

separated by cartilaginous pads (discs) that act as shock absorbers for the column. Nerves run out through the spinal cord to the periphery through openings in the vertebral bones. These nerves run very close to the discs, which is why protruding discs can cause pain along those nerves. As a result of an injury, an infection, or a genetic predisposition, the disc material can change consistency and produce pressure on the nerves that run out of the spinal cord. This pressure produces pain along those nerves.[4]

2. Have you ever heard of the *Sports Illustrated* Jinx? It seems that whenever a college football player is featured on the cover of *Sports Illustrated,* his performance on the field declines. This is nothing more than a simple example of regression to the mean. In a series of events an outstanding performance is likely to be followed by one that is more or less average.

3. Two new drugs—angiostatin and endostatin—have proved to be very effective in combating cancerous tumors in mice. The drugs are unique for two reasons. First, they are composed of natural substances the body makes, so they are less likely to cause side effects. Second, they stop the growth of cancer cells by an indirect method. The drugs eliminate the blood vessels to the tumor and the tumor dies because it is left without the nourishment and oxygen that the blood supply provides.

4. A new study has shown that live indoor plants may increase productivity and reduce stress. When people performed a simple task on a computer in a room with plants, their productivity increased 12 percent when compared with workers who performed the task in the same room without plants. Additionally, people tested in the presence of plants reported feeling about 10 percent more attentive after the task than those tested without plants present. Though no one is quite sure what accounts for this phenomenon, one researcher speculated that the presence of plants can lower blood pressure. By somehow causing us to be more relaxed, plants help us to be more productive and focused.

5. Cheap beer is a leading contributor to the spread of sexually transmitted diseases, according to a government report that says raising the tax on a six-pack by 20 cents could reduce gonorrhea by up to 9 percent. The Centers for Disease Control and Prevention study, released recently, compared changes in gonorrhea rates with changes in alcohol policy in all states from 1981 to 1996. In the years following beer tax increases, gonorrhea rates usually dropped among young people.

6. No one will ever build a flying vehicle that is capable of hovering high in the air while supported by nothing but magnetic fields. This applies to inhabitants of other planets as well. UFO enthusiasts often claim that the flying saucers they "observe" are held suspended in the air and obtain their propulsion from a self-generated magnetic field. However, it is not possible for a vehicle to hover, speed up, or change direction solely by

means of its own magnetic field. The proof of this lies in the fundamental principle of physics that nothing happens except through interactions between pairs of objects. A space vehicle may generate a powerful magnetic field, but in the absence of another magnetic field to push against, it can neither move nor support itself in midair. The earth possesses a magnetic field, but it is weak—about one percent of that generated by a compass needle. For a UFO to be levitated by reacting against the earth's magnetic field, its own field would have to be so enormously strong that it could be detected by any magnetometer in the world. And, finally, as the magnetic UFO traveled about the earth, it would induce electric currents in every power line within sight, blowing out circuit breakers and in general wreaking havoc. It would not go unnoticed.[5]

7.  As a boy swimming in the fundamentally rather chilly waters of Massachusetts Bay in summer, I discovered, as others had done before me, that for comfort in swimming, the water near the shore was apt to be warmer when the wind was blowing onshore—towards the shore—than when it was blowing offshore. By thoroughly unsystematic statistical methods I tested the discovery and found it to be true. But why should it be true? I shall try to give the essentials of what I believe to be the correct, though obvious, explanation, without spelling it out in all its logical, but boring, rigor.

    Warm water tends to rise. The sun warms the surface water more than the depths. For both reasons, surface water tends to be warmer than deeper water. The wind acts more on the surface water than it does on the depths, displacing it in the direction of the wind. Accordingly, the onshore wind tends to pile up the warmer water along the shore, while an offshore wind tends to move it away from the shore, where, by the principle that "water seeks its own level," it is continuously replaced by other water, which, since it can only come from the depths, must be relatively cold. Therefore, water along the shore tends to be warmer when the wind is blowing onshore than when it is blowing offshore.[6]

8.  Snow begins as rising mist from the ocean or dew from leaves. The molecules of water rise in the warming sunshine, bounding around. They rise as vapor until they are in the high cold air and the vapor molecules begin turning to solid water. One solid water molecule joins with another and then a third one comes along. Soon they form a six-sided figure. The molecules keep a six-sided pattern as they grow into a six-sided flake. Water molecules, made up of an oxygen and two hydrogen atoms, hold on to one another only in a certain way that always forms a hexagon.[7]

9.  **FLORIDA MOTHER ACCUSED OF MAKING DAUGHTER, 8, ILL**

    FORT LAUDERDALE, Fla.— Jennifer Bush, the Coral Springs, Fla. girl who spent much of her eight years beneath surgeon's knives, tethered to tubes and pumped full of medicine, will remain in state care until a judge decides whether the child's mother intentionally made her ill.

"We've got probable cause beyond question," Broward County Circuit Judge Arthur Birken said Tuesday as he ordered the state social-service agency to keep the child in protective custody. Birken quoted the child's psychologist who said taking Jennifer from her home would be the "safe" decision. Health officials and prosecutors believe her mother, Kathy, has Munchausen-by-proxy syndrome, a psychological condition in which a parent, usually a mother, purposely makes a child ill to get attention.[8]

10. In 1961, President John F. Kennedy, after meeting with his advisors, approved a CIA plan to invade Cuba (with 1400 Cuban exiles) and overthrow the government of Fidel Castro. The invasion, at the Bay of Pigs, was a total disaster. The invaders were killed or captured, the United States was humiliated, and Cuba moved politically closer to the Soviet Union. Why did the President and his advisors arrive at such a disastrous decision? Psychologists have long understood that group members who like each other and who share attitudes and interests—like a President and his most trusted advisors—often suffer from group think—the tendency, in close-knit groups, for all members to think alike and to suppress dissent and disagreement.[9]

11. Polar bears have evolved their white color as means of camouflage. You see, polar bears are predators and predators benefit from being concealed from their prey. Polar bears stalk seals resting on the ice. If the seal sees the bear coming from far away it can escape. And since the arctic environment is predominately white, the polar bear's white-colored fur serves as an effective means of camouflage.

12. A little known fact is that the Spanish influenza of 1918 killed millions and millions of people in less than a year. Nothing else—no infection, no war, no famine—has ever killed so many in such a short period. Why then did people pay so little attention to the epidemic in 1918 and why have they so thoroughly forgotten it since?

The very nature of the disease and its epidemiological characteristics encouraged forgetfulness in the societies it affected. The disease moved so fast, arrived, flourished, and was gone before it had any but ephemeral effects on the economy and before many people had the time to fully realize just how great was the danger. The enormous disparity between the flu's morbidity and mortality rates tended to calm potential victims. Which is more frightening, rabies, which strikes very few and, without proper treatment, kills them all, or Spanish influenza, which infects the majority and kills only two or three percent? For most people, the answer is rabies, without question.[10]

13. A softly glowing ball of light appears in the air nearby, hovers for a few seconds, passes through an object and then vanishes. It's a phenomenon known as ball lightning, which appears during thunderstorms as a luminous sphere about the size of an orange or grapefruit.

Observers have reported seeing ball lightning for centuries, only to be greeted with skepticism. Now, two physicists from the Universidad

Complutense in Madrid, Spain, describe a possible explanation for ball lightning; something called an "electromagnetic knot," in which lines of an electric or magnetic field join to form a closed knot.

The researchers say the lines of force are powerful enough to trap a lump of the glowing, hot, electrically charged gas that can be created in a thunderstorm. Temperatures in the ball may reach more than 50,000 degrees Fahrenheit. But the energy soon dissipates, the knot untangles, and the luminous ball disappears into thin air.

14. Societies without exception exert strong cultural sanctions against incest. Sociobiologist E. O. Wilson posits the existence of what he terms, "a far deeper, less rational form of enforcement," which he regards as genetic.

Because of recessive genes, children of incest carry a higher risk than others of mental retardation, physical deformity, and early death; they are, therefore, less likely to mate and reproduce than are children of parents who avoid incest. Hence, individuals with a genetic inclination against incest contribute more genes to succeeding generations.

15. The availability of jobs in just about every profession is bound to ebb and flow. Today there is a demand for teachers and a glut of nurses. A decade ago, the situation was just the reverse— too many unemployed teachers and not enough nurses. This is all due to the fact that people tend to opt for training in areas where jobs are currently available. As more and more people in that area come into the job market, the number of candidates for jobs exceeds the number of available jobs. Hence, fewer and fewer people opt to train in that area, with the net result that within a few years there are not enough trained professionals to fill the available jobs. When this happens, more people elect to train in the underemployed area and the cycle repeats itself.

*Exercises 16–25 all contain explanations. For each, come up with at least one rival explanation and then, using Ockham's Razor, try to decide which is most likely to be correct.*

*(Note: On page 51 a solution is provided for Exercise 16.)*

16. Thinking about quitting school for the sake of your mental health? Think again. College graduates across the nation feel better emotionally and physically than high school dropouts because they have better jobs, take better care of themselves, and have better access to health care. A recent survey released by the Centers for Disease Control and Prevention found that college graduates felt healthy an average of 26 days a month while high school dropouts felt good 22.8 days a month.

17. Academy award winners live nearly four years longer than their colleagues, according to a study that credits the effect of an Academy Award on an actor's self esteem. "Once you get the Oscar, it gives you an inner sense of peace and accomplishment that can last for your entire life and that alters the way your body copes with stress on a day-to-day basis," says Donald A. Redeimeier, a professor of medicine at the University of Toronto. Redeimeier found that Oscar

winners live nearly four years longer than either actors who were never nominated or those who were nominated but did not win. Multiple winners are even more fortunate, living an average of six years longer than their silver-screen counterparts.

18. A scientist who studies vision and the brain has made a curious discovery about portrait painting. Artists almost always place one eye of their subject at the horizontal center of the picture. Dr. Christopher Tyler took photos of 170 famous portraits from the past five centuries and marked the midpoint along the horizontal top of the picture. Then he drew a straight vertical line that divided each painting at its horizontal center. To his astonishment, one eye or the other almost always fell on or near the horizontal center. In talking to art experts, Tyler found that none knew of any rule for placing an eye at the horizontal center. He concluded that artists must be doing it unconsciously as the result of some intuitive sense of the aesthetic appeal of this arrangement.

19. Recently, a new product was introduced called The Laundry Solution. It consisted of a hard plastic ball filled with a blue liquid. Though the ball costs $75, its makers claim that you will never need to buy laundry soap again. Just put the miracle ball in the washing machine with your laundry and everything will come clean without the need for soap! It seems that the ball contains specially structured water that emits a negative charge through the walls of the container into your laundry water. This causes the water molecule cluster to disassociate, allowing much smaller individual water molecules to penetrate into the innermost parts of the fabric.

20. A study done recently at Purdue University found that religious people are more likely to be overweight than nonreligious people. In state-by-state comparisons, obesity was found to be the highest in states where religious affiliation was more prevalent. Michigan, Mississippi, and Indiana were among the states with the highest percentage of overweight persons. Likewise, obesity figures were lower in states that had the least number of religious persons. Those included Massachusetts, Hawaii, and Colorado. The author of the study, Sociology Professor Kenneth Ferraro, speculated that American churches are virtually silent on excess body weight, despite a Biblical dictate for moderation in all things. Though gluttony is listed as a sign of moral weakness, few religious groups have any proscriptions against overeating.

21. You've probably heard or seen stories about people who are able to walk over red-hot beds of coals. It seems that if you can focus all of your powers of concentration you can will your body not to feel the pain and to be immune to the damage the hot coals might otherwise cause.

22. Although the connection between conscious and unconscious thoughts have remained obscure, psychologists theorize that a link exists. Now scientists have apparently provided some proof: the first physiological evidence that unconscious brain processes can control a seemingly voluntary act. The

researchers found that the brain signals initiating muscle movement for clenching the fist begin before a person becomes aware of deciding to do it. Benjamin Libet, a psychologist at the University of California, asked five subjects to clench their fists whenever they felt like it. The subjects remembered when they became conscious of the desire to do so by watching a special clock that enabled them to note the time to within a fraction of a second. Meanwhile, the researchers monitored the subjects' brains for a kind of electrical activity called the readiness potential that changes just before a person is about to use a muscle. Libet found that the readiness potential always changed about a third of a second before subjects were aware of the decision to clench their fists.

23. A recent telephone survey of 113,000 Americans about religious affiliation came up with some rather interesting facts. Perhaps the most interesting was that, while nationwide 7.5 percent of the respondents said they belonged to no church, 15 percent of the sampled residents of Oregon, Washington, and California claimed no religious affiliation. It seems clear that all the "new age" mumbo jumbo that goes on out west is turning people away from God.

24. The following story appeared about an advertisement in a weekly news magazine as well as in the local newspapers. It seems that the Pepsi-Cola Company decided that Coke's three-to-one lead in Dallas, Texas was no longer acceptable, so they commissioned a taste preference study. The participants were chosen from Coke drinkers in the Dallas area and asked to express a preference for a glass of Coke or a glass of Pepsi. The glasses were not labeled "Coke" and "Pepsi" because of the obvious bias that might be associated with a cola's brand name. Rather, in an attempt to administer the two drinks in a blind fashion, the Coke glass was simply marked with a "Q" and the Pepsi glass with an "M." Results indicated that more than half chose Pepsi over Coke. It seems clear that, when the effects of advertising are set aside, cola drinkers prefer the taste of Pepsi to Coke.[11]

25. From time to time, one hears stories of strange, almost unbelievable animal behavior. Pets, for example, seem to sense when their masters are about to return. Dogs and cats have been known to move their young to a safe place just before an earthquake. There are many documented cases in which animals have reacted strangely to their impending death or that of their masters. These incidents involve knowledge that came to the animals in some apparently paranormal way. There is no apparent explanation for them—except ESP.

## A SOLUTION TO EXERCISE 1

a. *What is being explained?* The manner in which a protruding disc can cause nerve pain.

b. *What is the explanation?* Nerves run very close to discs and when discs are injured, infected, etc., they can change consistency and protrude. This in turn causes pressure on the nerves, which results in pain.

c. *What if any recognizable sorts of explanatory claims occur in the explanation?* The passage explains a disc problem can cause nerve pain. It does so by discussing the intervening causal mechanism: the sequence of events, beginning with damage to a disc and ending in lower back nerve pain. The passage also gives a functional explanation of the vertebral discs: they serve as a kind of shock absorber.

## A SOLUTION TO EXERCISE 16

*One possible rival explanation is that college graduates are more likely to exaggerate when asked to assess their own condition than are high school dropouts, so that the results we are trying to explain are largely illusory. The explanation in the passage seems more in keeping with Ockham's Razor. Access to health care and job success and contentment seem to be just the sorts of things that would contribute to a sense of personal well-being. By contrast, it seems more than a little odd to suggest that a tendency to exaggerate increases with education. Why on earth should this be the case?*

## NOTES

1. This example is adapted from *Nuts and Bolts for the Social Sciences,* by Jon Elster, a very readable account of prominent causal mechanisms used in the social scientific explanation.

2. The studies on which this example is based describe the situation before a vaccine for hepatitis B was developed. It is interesting to note that before the advent of the vaccine, chances of dying from accidental exposure to hepatitis B were almost identical to those today associated with accidental exposure to HIV. Yet the hepatitis B risk received much less attention than that given today to accidental HIV exposure in the medical community.

3. The use of "razor" here derives from the fact that Ockham used his principle to "shave away" certain metaphysical entities in which philosophers of the time generally believed. Ockham used the razor, for example, to argue that abstractions are not "real" things over and above the words used to express them. One can, on Ockham's view, account for the significance of such expressions without introducing the notion of corresponding abstract entities.

4. Hister, Art. *Dr. Art Hister's Do-it-yourself Guide to Good Health.* Toronto: Random House, 1990, p. 178.

5. Rothmman, Milton A. *A Physicist's Guide to Skepticism.* Buffalo: Prometheus Books, 1988, pp. 148–149.

6. Homas, George. *The Nature of Social Science.* New York: Harcourt, Brace & World, 1967, p. 21.

7. Marvin, Rob. "What in the World." *The Oregoninan,* Jan. 21, 1993.

8. Donna Leinwand. Knight-Ridder News Service, in *The Oregonian,* Apr. 17, 1996.

9. Adopted from Wade and Tavris. *Psychology,* 2nd ed. New York: Harper Collins, 1990.

10. Crosby, Alfred W. *America's Forgotten Pandemic: The Influenza of 1918.* Cambridge: Cambridge, 1989, p. 321.

11. Adapted from a case study in Huck, Schuyler W., and Sandler, Howard M. *Rival Hypotheses.* New York: Harper & Row, 1976.

# 4

# Testing Explanations

## THE BASIC METHOD

Suppose we've made a set of observations and have uncovered something unusual. We have our suspicions about what might explain it but we are not sure. Now, we need to find a way to test our suspicions. In this chapter we will introduce the basic strategy involved in scientific tests. Then, in Chapter 5 we will focus on the way this strategy plays out in one very common and important type of scientific research—studies designed to investigate large scale causal relationships.

How do we go about putting an explanation to the test? The basic strategy is really very simple. We begin by trying to find something that ought to happen if the explanation is correct. Suppose I've just flipped the switch on my desk lamp and nothing has happened. My guess is that the bulb is burned out. If I'm right, then it follows that if I remove the bulb I ought to be able to spot a break in its filament. Next, I check the bulb to see if I am right. If the filament is ruptured, I've confirmed my suspicions. However, if the bulb is in working order I now have evidence that my explanation is wrong. Something else must be causing the problem. This simple strategy—making and testing a prediction, associated with an explanation—is at the heart of the method by which ideas are put to the test in science.

As we shall soon see, however, explanation testing is rarely as straightforward as in the case we just considered. It may be difficult to settle on a prediction that can provide unambiguous evidence for an explanation. Unlike our example, moreover, we cannot test every explanation by simply looking to see what is the case in the natural world. Often, the testing of an explanation requires the creation of artificially imposed circumstances designed specifically to yield a decisive prediction. The net result is that a great deal of effort is often required to design and execute a competent scientific test. To get a grasp of the problems that may be encountered in designing and carrying out an experiment, let's look at a few case studies from the world of science. Along the way, we will set forth two criteria that any good scientific test satisfy.

## HOW TO TEST AN EXPLANATION

One of the more interesting episodes in the history of science involves the theory of spontaneous generation. As recently as the late 1800s many people believed that living organisms could be generated from nonliving material. One physician in the seventeenth century, for example, claimed that mice arose from a dirty shirt and a few grains of wheat placed in a dark corner. Similarly, it was thought that maggots—tiny white wormlike creatures, the larval stage of common houseflies—were generated spontaneously out of decaying food. In 1688, an Italian physician, Francesca Redi, published a work in which he challenged the doctrine that decaying meat will eventually turn into flies. The following passage is from Redi's *Experiments in the Generation of Insects:*

> . . . I began to believe that all worms found in meat were derived directly from the droppings of flies, and not from the putrefaction of meat, and I was still more confirmed in this belief by having observed that, before the meat grew wormy, flies had hovered over it, of the same kind as those that later bred in it. Belief would be vain without the confirmation of experiment, hence in the middle of July I put a snake, some fish, some eels from the Arno and a slice of milk-fed veal in four large wide-mouthed flasks; having well closed and sealed them, I then filled the same number of flasks in the same way, only leaving these open.[1]

In this passage Redi does a number of things. He tells us of the observations that led him to his explanatory hypothesis and then gives us his explanation. Next, he describes the test he carried out. Though he doesn't explicitly set forth his prediction, it seems clear from what he says. Here are the various elements of his test:

*Explanation:* worms (maggots) are derived directly from the droppings of flies.

*Experimental conditions:* two sets of flasks are filled with meat or fish. One set is sealed and the other is left open so that flies can enter.

*Prediction:* worms will appear only in the second set of flasks.

Is Redi's test a good one? Is it, in other words, sufficiently well designed to enable him to decide whether his explanation is correct? To answer these questions, we need to look at the conclusions we would be justified in drawing given the experiment's two possible outcomes.

Consider first what follows if the predicted result fails to occur—if worms appear in the sealed flasks as well, or if there are no worms in either set. Are we entitled to reject Redi's hypothesis? The answer here is not as clear as it may seem. What, for example, if the seals were not perfect? Perhaps then flies may have contaminated the sealed containers. Or what if flies for some reason did not lay eggs in the unsealed flasks? If either of these possibilities is the case, it may be that Redi's hypothesis is right after all. So we can reject Redi's explanation, but only provided we have no reason to suspect anything has happened to compromise the experiment, anything, that is, like the two possibilities above. One feature of a well designed experiment, then, is that it will take sufficient precautions to ensure that the prediction ought to occur if the explanation is right. If the sealed flasks have not been compromised, and if both sets were exposed to sufficient numbers of flies, Redi's experiment meets what we might call the _falsifiability criterion:_

> A good test will be designed to rule out factors that could account for a failed prediction even if the explanation is correct.

If this criterion is met, an experiment will enable us to reject a faulty explanation. If we are sure that something will happen if the explanation is right, and if that something fails to occur, we can conclude that the explanation must be wrong. Though we can hardly expect to anticipate all of the things that could go wrong in designing and carrying out an experiment, it is always worthwhile to pause and think about potential problems that might compromise the results. For example, in any experiment involving an apparatus (like Redi's flasks) we would do well to make sure the apparatus is operating properly.

Consider next what follows if the predicted result occurs. In fact, Redi did get the results he expected. The passage continues:

> It was not long before the meat and fish, in these second vessels, became wormy and flies were seen entering and leaving at will; but in the closed flasks I did not see a worm though many days had passed since the dead flesh had been put in them.

Has Redi established his explanation? Can we be sure the worms are due to fly droppings? Once again, the answer requires a bit of qualification. Before we embrace Redi's explanation, we must be sure that nothing else—other than fly droppings—could account for his results. Many scientists of Redi's time believed in the doctrine of spontaneous generation and looked upon his results with some suspicion. They speculated that there might be some "active principle" in the air necessary for spontaneous generation. By depriving the meat and fish in the sealed containers of a sufficient flow of fresh air, they reasoned, Redi may have inadvertently prevented the spontaneous generation of worms. Thus, it seems at least a possibility that Redi's explanation is wrong even though his prediction turned out to be right.

In light of this objection, Redi modified his experiment. Rather than sealing the first set of flasks, he covered them with a "fine Naples veil" that kept

*control*
*placebo*
*time*
*population*

---

**QUICK REVIEW 4.1    Falsifiability and Verifiability**

To be well designed, an experiment must meet two criteria:

Falsifiability-A good test will rule out factors that could account for a failed prediction even if the explanation is right.

Verifiability-A good test will rule out factors that could explain a

successful prediction if the explanation is wrong.

A test that does not meet the falsifiability criterion cannot reject an explanation. One that does not meet the verifiability criterion cannot confirm an explanation.

---

flies from coming into contact with the meat and fish but did allow air to circulate. Carrying out this modified experiment Redi once again obtained the expected results: worms appeared only in the covered flasks. By this maneuver Redi was able to rule out the possibility that some something in the air might be responsible for his results. As a result, the conclusion that fly droppings were responsible for the worms was on a much stronger footing. The modification Redi needed to make to test his explanation suggests a second criterion that a decisive explanatory test must satisfy:

A good test will be designed to accommodate factors that could account for a successful prediction, even if the explanation is wrong.

This second requirement is called the *verifiability criterion* because we cannot accept a test as having verified an explanation unless we have good reason to believe that nothing else could have accounted for the predicted result.

In tests of causal explanations like Redi's, experimental and control groups will often be used to satisfy the verifiability criterion. The members of the two groups will differ in only one respect. The experimental group but not the control group will be subject to the suspected cause. (In such experiments, the suspected cause will sometimes be called the independent variable and its claimed effect, the dependent variable.) The prediction, then, will be that only members of the experimental group will respond in the appropriate way. Thus, in Redi's second test, the experimental group was composed of the bits of meat and fish in the veil-covered flasks and the control specimens were those in the open flasks. His prediction was that worms would be found only in the latter group, the open flasks. Control groups provide an effective counter to the nagging possibility that some unknown explanatory factor may have been overlooked, something that may account for a successful outcome even if the explanation is wrong. For if the experimental and control groups are identical it is hard to imagine some factor other than the suspected cause that could be responsible for the predicted difference in outcomes between the two groups.

One further feature of Redi's work is worth noting. Under naturally occurring conditions it would probably have been impossible to isolate specimens of meat and fish having absolutely no contact with flies. To test his explanation

Redi found it necessary to put his specimens in a somewhat unnatural environment. But explanation testing does not always involve the kind of contrived, "laboratory" conditions required by Redi. Sometimes nature will provide the clues necessary to test an explanation. Consider, for example, the test described in the following news story.

*Satellite Supports "Big Bang" Theory*

Phoenix—A NASA satellite has provided powerful evidence supporting the "big bang" theory, which holds that the universe began over 15 billion years ago with the most colossal explosion ever.

John C. Mather, an astronomer with the space agency, said Thursday that precise measurements by the Cosmic Background Explorer satellite of the remnant energy from the big bang given readings that are exactly as the theory predicted.

The theory, first aired in the 1920s, posits that all matter in the universe was once compressed into an exceedingly small and super-heated center that exploded, sending energy and particles outward uniformly in all directions. At the moment of the explosion, temperatures would have been trillions and trillions of degrees and have been cooling ever since.

If the theory is correct, astronomers expected an even distribution of temperatures just fractionally above absolute zero to still exist in the universe as an afterglow from the explosion.

Mather said that a Cobe instrument called the Far Infrared Absolute Spectrophotometer has now taken hundreds of millions of measurements across the full sky and has determined that the primordial temperatures are uniformly distributed. He said the uniform temperature left from the big bang is 2.726 degrees above absolute zero—or about minus 456.9 degrees F.[2]

This story reports on the results of an experiment done to provide new evidence for an explanation most astronomers and cosmologists accept: the big bang theory. (Even the most well entrenched explanations can benefit from further confirmation, particularly if they involve elements—like the big bang theory—that cannot be directly observed.) The theory predicts a uniform temperature throughout the universe and consists of millions of measurements taken across the full sky.

Now, this experiment clearly satisfies the falsifiability criterion, unless we have some reason to suspect the apparatus used to take the measurements. If the big bang theory is right, there should be a uniform afterglow and it ought to be detectable using the techniques mentioned. But does it meet the verifiability condition? Can we, in other words, rule out the possibility that something else might explain the predicted result? Perhaps not, if the prediction were simply that there should be a uniform temperature throughout the universe. Other cosmological theories might be able to account for the uniformity. Or a successful match between prediction and actual outcome may be a matter of happenstance. After all, the universe either has a uniform background temperature or it does not. Perhaps the match was just a bit of luck. But the actual prediction involves a bit more. The story goes on to say:

Craig Hogan, a University of Washington astronomer, said the new research "is verifying the textbooks" by providing powerful evidence for the theory. Hogan said that the Cobe results exactly match the theoretical curve of temperature energy decay that would be expected in the big bang theory.

This new passage suggests the verifiability condition is met, largely because of the specificity of the prediction. The big bang theory predicts a very specific temperature at a very specific time in the development of the universe. And, as it turns out, the universe is just as advertised. The close fit between prediction and experimental outcome would be hard to explain if the big bang theory were wrong!

Natural observations can also yield evidence that an explanation may be wrong. Here is another recent news story pertaining, coincidentally, to the big bang theory:

*Discovery Offers Fresh Insight into Makeup of Universe*

Astronomers have discovered a pair of collapsed stars, remnants of catastrophic supernova explosions, that may be composed entirely of free quarks, the never before observed building blocks of the protons and neutrons that make up normal matter. The discoveries imply that long-standing theories governing how stars die when their nuclear fuel is exhausted need a major overhaul to explain the existence of "strange quark stars," the last possible step before the ultimate collapse into a black hole.[3]

The story describes the work of David Helfand, an astronomer at Columbia University, using NASA's Chandra X-Ray Observatory. Helfand examined a spinning pulsar 10,000 light years away known as 3C58. The story goes on:

Neutron stars cool off by radiating tiny particles called neutrinos. After 10 years, such a star's temperature should be about 5 million degrees. After that, it cools more slowly. Given its age, Helfand expected the temperature of 3C58 to be a bit less than 2 million degrees. "Our observations show in the case of this remnant that the temperature is far lower than that and the energy being radiated is down by at least a factor of 10 from what was expected," he said. "This observation requires a fundamental revision in our models of the structure and evolution of neutron stars."

Prevailing "models of the structure and evolution of neutron stars" predict the temperature of 3C58 should be a bit less than 2 million degrees. But the measurements taken by Helfand suggest its temperature is much lower. The received explanation—the currently accepted model—predicts a certain temperature, but observation reveals that the predicted result is quite wrong. If there is no way of accounting for this discrepancy as an artifact of the techniques used to make the measurements, this experiment makes quite a strong case against the prevailing model.

It is rare for a big idea in science to be verified or falsified by the results of a single experiment. Typically, the results of one test will provide tentative

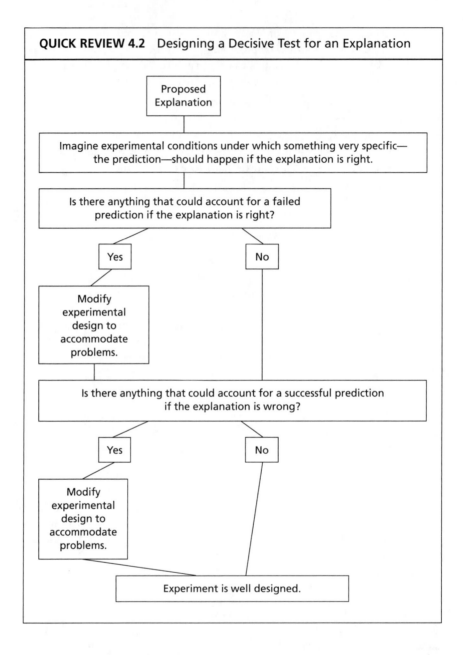

**QUICK REVIEW 4.2**  Designing a Decisive Test for an Explanation

Proposed Explanation

Imagine experimental conditions under which something very specific—the prediction—should happen if the explanation is right.

Is there anything that could account for a failed prediction if the explanation is right?

Yes / No

Modify experimental design to accommodate problems.

Is there anything that could account for a successful prediction if the explanation is wrong?

Yes / No

Modify experimental design to accommodate problems.

Experiment is well designed.

evidence and point in the direction of needed further experimentation, much as Redi's initial experiment pointed to the need for a further experiment involving free flowing air. Even after Redi had confirmed his explanation, much remained to be done. Building on the work of Redi and others, later researchers were able to look much deeper into the phenomenon Redi had documented. Their work made use of a new scientific instrument, the microscope, to observe the behavior of bacteria and other microorganisms to refine the explanatory ideas developed by Redi. Similarly, the negative results of a single test will rarely be sufficient to overturn an explanation, especially if it has been well confirmed by previous experimental results. No doubt current ideas about the structure and evolution of neutron stars will be modified in light of the experimental results discussed above. But the larger theory of which it is a part—the big bang theory—will remain intact though slightly modified to reflect these results.

## HOW NOT TO TEST AN EXPLANATION

We have said that a decisive test must satisfy two criteria—falsifiability and verifiability. Perhaps the most effective way to underscore their importance is by looking at an experiment in which neither is satisfied. The experiment described in the following passage is intended to shed light on the question of whether or not animals have ESP.

> At mealtime you might put out two feedpans instead of one for your dog or cat. The feedpans should be located so that they are equally convenient to the animal. They should be placed six to eight inches apart. Both should contain the same amount of food and avoid using a feedpan the animal is familiar with. Pick the dish you wish the animal to eat from and concentrate on it. In this test, the animal has a 50% chance of choosing correctly half the time. You may want to keep a record of his responses over several weeks to determine how well your pet has done.[4]

The explanation under scrutiny here is that animals are receptive to human thoughts via ESP and the prediction is that, under the experimental conditions outlined, pets will pick the dish we are thinking of more than 50 percent of the time. (Not a 50 percent chance "half the time" as the author of the passage claims!)

Is the test described in the passage a good one? First we must ask whether it meets the falsifiability condition. Is there anything that could account for a failed prediction if the explanation is true? Suppose you were to say to your pet, in an entirely monotonous tone of voice, "Eat out of the red dish, the dish on the left, Fido." I doubt Fido would grasp the meaning of your words. Domestic animals tend to react to a complex of behavioral cues, some given by vocal inflection, but not to the meaning of words uttered in their presence. Thus if saying aloud, "eat out of the red dish" will not do the trick, it is doubtful that thinking the same thing silently will work. Nor will it do to "picture" in your "mind's eye" the red bowl. I doubt Fido would react in the appropriate way to an actual picture of the bowl, so it seems highly unlikely Fido would react to nothing more than a "mental picture" of the red bowl. Thus, under the experimental conditions described in the passage, it seems entirely possible that Fido may fail even if he or she has some incipient extrasensory powers. A failed prediction, then, would not entitle us to conclude that animals do not have ESP unless we are willing to grant the entirely dubious claim that animals can understand human thoughts and words.

Does the test satisfy the verifiability condition? Is there anything that could account for a successful outcome if the explanation is false? A number of things come to mind here that might explain a successful outcome. First, suppose that our subject tended to go to one bowl instead of the other. It is possible that the experimenter, who is both sending the instructions and observing the outcome, will inadvertently think of the dish the pet favors. Second, domestic animals are very good at discerning nonverbal cues. It may be that the experimenter is inadvertently looking at or standing in the direction of the dish being thought about and the experimental subject is picking up these cues. Finally there may be some bias at work on the part of the experimenter. Suppose our experimenter were convinced in advance of doing the experiment that animals have ESP. In recording or evaluating the subject's responses, the experimenter might inadvertently leave out responses that would otherwise provide evidence against animal ESP.

As you can see, the experimental test sketched in the passage is poorly designed in that it will enable us to conclude neither that pets do or do not have ESP. The kind of analysis we have just completed should be done as a part of the design of any experiment. If our first attempts at designing an experiment fail to satisfy our two criteria we can go back to the drawing board armed with what we have discovered about potential weaknesses. Our subsequent design efforts are bound to do a more effective job of satisfying our two criteria.

## TESTING EXTRAORDINARY CLAIMS

With a few modifications, the experimental strategy used to test explanations can be used to test extraordinary claims of the sort discussed in Chapter 2. Consider one such claim. People, known as "water witches" or "dowsers" claim they can detect water with a simple forked wooden branch. Dowsers loosely grasp one of the forks in each hand and point the branch straight ahead, parallel to the ground. When they approach a source of water, the dowsing rod, as the forked stick is called, will point in the direction of the water, much as a compass needle will point in the direction of magnetic north. Many successful dowsers claim to be able to pinpoint sources of water for purposes of well drilling and some even claim to have found water where conventional geologists have failed.

As with most extraordinary claims, the evidence for dowsing is sketchy. We must rely on the testimony of dowsers and their clients about past performances. Moreover, the fact that a dowser, say, points to a location, a well is drilled and water discovered does not show that the dowser actually located water with his or her dowsing rod. That water was found at the indicated location may have been a coincidence, or there may have been visual clues to aid the dowser—patches of greenery near the chosen location, etc. And we have no real sense of dowsers' success rates, other than what they and their clients report. How often are they mistaken? Our challenge, then, is to devise an experiment that will give us decisive evidence, one way or the other, about the dowser's claimed ability.

To satisfy the falsifiability condition, we need to come up with a set of conditions under which nothing could explain a dowser's failure other than an inability to find water with a dowsing rod. A good rule of thumb in setting up tests of extraordinary claims is to consult the experimental subject or subjects prior to designing the experiment. We want to set up conditions under which the experimental subjects will agree, in advance, that they ought to be able to perform. Otherwise failure in the actual test may be taken to show only that the experiment is hostile to the ability we are attempting to test. But if our subjects concur that the experiment approximates conditions under which they should be able to perform, such excuses lose much of their steam. If a person says he or she can perform under a given set of conditions, it is hard to take seriously protestations to the contrary particularly after a failed test.

To satisfy the verifiability condition we need experimental conditions under which nothing could explain our subject's success other than a real ability to dowse. What we want to try to rule out is the possibility of cheating, coincidence, inadvertent cuing on our part, visual or audio clues as to where the water is, and the like. If we succeed in imposing controls sufficiently tight to rule out these possibilities, success by the dowser can be taken to vindicate his or her claimed extraordinary ability.

Now that we have a sense of what a good experiment ought to involve, let's try our hand at actually designing one. Imagine we have contacted a group of the country's most well known and successful dowsers and all have agreed to take part in our experiment. We propose the following test. We will place before each dowser ten identical large ceramic jars with covers, arranged in a straight line equidistant from one another. Only one of the jars will contain water. The other nine will be empty. The dowser will be allowed to approach each jar but not to touch any jar. We will only test subjects who agree that they should be able to find the single jar with water. (We might give them a chance to dowse a jar they know contains water to insure that the experimental conditions meet their approval.) If a dowser is successful, he or she will be retested once the jars are rearranged. Of course, our subject will be asked to leave the room while the jars are being rearranged. As an additional precaution, no one who knows the location of the jar containing water will be allowed to be in the room while a dowser is being tested.

With all of the precautions we have built in, our experiment is well designed to provide unambiguous results. If a dowser can perform under such conditions we have strong evidence for dowsing. The odds of choosing the right jar in the first run are one in ten, in the first and the second, one in a hundred. It is hard to imagine anything other than dowsing that could explain such results in our tightly controlled experiment. If, instead, the dowsers fail, it would be hard to explain away the results given that the subjects have agreed that they should be able to perform under the test conditions.

One feature of our test deserves special note. We have been careful to arrive at a prediction that sets a clear line of demarcation between success and failure.

If our dowser can find the jar containing water in two successive trials, he or she is successful; anything less constitutes failure. In designing controlled tests it is important to avoid predictions that blur the line between success and failure. Imagine, for example, we had decided to test our dowser by burying containers of water a few feet below the surface of a vacant lot. The dowser would then be instructed to place markers where he or she believed the containers to be located. Suppose the dowser placed markers within three or four feet of the location of one of the containers. Does this constitute a hit or a miss? Just how far off must a marker be before we consider it a miss? Or suppose markers are placed at ten locations when only five containers were buried and that seven of the markers are within a few feet of one or the other of the containers. How do we evaluate these results? Has our dowser succeeded or failed?

The line between success and failure can be very difficult to draw when a prediction involves some sort of subjective impression on the part of the experimental subject. Imagine, for example, we were to test a telepath—someone who claims to be able to read the thoughts of another. As part of our experiment we instruct the telepath to sketch a simple picture that someone in another room is concentrating on. Suppose the person in the other room is looking at a postcard of a small sailboat moored at a marina and that the telepath produces a simple drawing that includes a vertical straight line and a narrow triangular shape that might correspond to a boat hull or sail. To make matters worse, several of the drawing's details conform clearly to nothing we can discern on the postcard. Is the telepath's impression accurate or inaccurate? Presuming we can decide what constitutes a detail or feature of the picture on the card, how many features or details must the telepath get right to be a clear indication of success?

To take another example, imagine a tarot card reader were to give a personality analysis, based on the position and order of the cards, of someone unknown to the reader. The reading might indicate that the person in question, say, "tends to be optimistic despite occasional moments of depression or pessimism" or "makes friends easily" or "displays clear leadership ability." How do we evaluate such claims? The problem here is not only with the generality of the predictions but with the lack of a clear basis for judging them. We must first arrive at an accurate personality profile of the person in question. Presuming we could do this, what objective basis do we have for comparing our profile with that of the tarot card reader? No doubt any two sets of subjective impressions about a person's character will contain some words and phrases in common. How much similarity is required to put some stock in the analysis of the tarot card reader?

In designing a test, then, it is crucial that we arrive at a prediction that clearly spells out the difference between success and failure. If in evaluating the results of a test we are unable to say precisely whether our subject has succeeded or failed, then our test has very little point. Fortunately, however, the prediction in our dowsing test seems to be clear and unequivocal; success and failure are clearly spelled out.

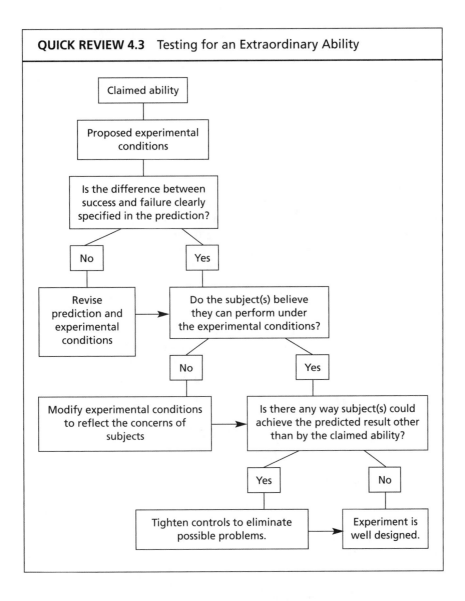

QUICK REVIEW 4.3    Testing for an Extraordinary Ability

No matter how well they are designed, tests of extraordinary abilities face a further difficulty. Suppose we run our test and all of our dowsers fail. Believers in dowsing are likely to explain away our results on the ground that we have tested the wrong people, that our experiment is flawed in ways neither we nor they understand, or even that dowsing only works "in the field" under noncontrolled conditions. They will probably go on to point out that dowsing has been practiced for hundreds of years; the earliest record of a successful dowsing dates to 1586, in Spain. Such objections are nearly impossible to counter, but for this reason they lack any real credibility. They boil down to nothing more than the claim that dowsing cannot be tested. We need only reply that if it cannot be tested, then we have no reason to believe it works! Dowsing is something of an anomaly and as we found in Chapter 2, the burden of proof lies with the believer, not the skeptic. Lacking any clear experimental evidence for dowsing, then, it is reasonable to assume that dowsing does not work.

## SUMMARY

The basic strategy used to test an explanation is always the same. Isolate a prediction that will occur if an explanation is correct. Tests can be undertaken under laboratory conditions where circumstances will be arranged to yield a prediction, or in the real world by checking the prediction against the facts. In either case, the prediction must enable us to reject the explanation if it is wrong and to confirm it if it is correct. To accomplish this, any experiment must satisfy two criteria. First, it must rule out factors that could account for predictive failure even if the explanation is correct (the falsifiability criterion). Second, it must rule out factors that could explain predictive success even if the explanation is wrong (the verifiability criterion). By a similar experimental strategy, extraordinary claims and abilities can be tested. In such a test, care must be taken to insure that the predicted outcome is clear and measurable and that the subject or subjects believe they can perform under the conditions specified.

## EXERCISES

*Exercises 1–10 involve explanations and extraordinary claims or abilities. For each, design a decisive test, that is, one that satisfies both the verifiability and falsifiability criteria. In the case of extraordinary claims and abilities, particularly, make sure the predicted difference between success and failure is clear and measurable. Be prepared to modify your first efforts when you begin to think seriously about factors that might compromise the integrity of your results.*

*(NOTE: A solution is provided for Exercise 1 on page 68. Look it over carefully to get a sense of how to solve the other problems.)*

1.  Recently I have noticed something peculiar and really quite irritating about my doctor. If my appointment is for early in the day, I usually see my doctor within a few minutes of the appointed time. But when my appointment is later in the day, I've spent as much as an extra hour sitting in the waiting room or waiting in the examination room. I think I know what the problem is. Whenever I come in for an appointment, my doctor insists on catching up on the details of my life; he asks about my work, my family, how much I'm exercising, even if I've seen any interesting movies or read any good books lately. It seem to me clear that my doctor spends way too much time

"chatting" with his clients about things not related to the problem they are there to see him about. As a result, he falls further and further behind as the day goes on.

2. A fact of life in large organizations—whether in the private or the public sector—is that an enormous number of people are doing jobs for which they are not qualified. This is because of what is often called "The Peter Principle." People tend to rise to the level of their incompetency. In a large organization, if you are good at what you do, you will be promoted. And if you are competent at your new job you will be promoted once again. The process of advancement stops only when a person rises to a position where they are not fully competent. Lacking competency they will do a poor job and thus not be promoted further. So a person's final position in a large organization will be a position they are not qualified to fill.

3. Many of you have probably played with a Ouija board. On a rectangular board approximately 2 feet by 3 feet are printed all of the letters of the alphabet, the numbers from 1–10 and the words, "yes" and "no." A small, plastic three legged stool, called the planchette, is placed on the Ouija board. Two people, sitting on opposite sides of the board, rest the tips of their fingers gently on opposite ends of the planchette. Somebody then asks the spirit of the Ouija board a question and what follows is startling. The planchette slowly begins to move, and will often spell out an answer to the question! What is more, the answer is frequently something that neither of the participants have any way of knowing. The spirit may even predict something that is yet to happen. As anybody who has played with the Ouija board will attest, one has the distinct feeling that the planchette is actually pulling the hands of the participants about the board; the participants do not feel as though they are pushing the planchette. Well, this is just wrong. In fact the participants are moving the planchette. The eerie feeling of being dragged about the board results from the fact that each participant is exerting only half as much effort as it would take a single person to move the planchette. The resulting impression—that something else is doing the work—is thus understandable. But this "something else" is not the spirit of the Ouija. It is the person on the other end of the planchette.

4. A recent telephone survey of 113,000 Americans about religious affiliation came up with some rather interesting facts. Perhaps the most interesting was that while nationwide, 7.5 percent of the respondents said they belonged to no church, 15 percent of the sampled residents of Oregon, Washington, and California claimed no religious affiliation. It seems clear that all the "new age" mumbo jumbo that goes on out west is turning people away from God.

5. Recently, a good friend quit her job. This is surprising because her income was in the six-figure

range as a partner at a large law firm. And guess what she is doing now? She sold her home, and bought a tiny, primitive cabin in the woods where she lives alone and claims to be studying to become a Buddhist monk! She says she has enough money put away to live for a year or so and afterwards doesn't know what she is going to do. This amazes me because she has always been such a responsible person. You know what I think? She's undergoing a good, old fashioned midlife crisis.

6. Exercise 24 in Chapter 3 (pg. 50) involved a taste test to determine whether cola drinkers preferred Pepsi to Coke. In the test, glasses containing Coke were marked with a "Q" and those containing Pepsi with an "M." My guess is that the reason subjects preferred Pepsi by a three to one margin was because of an unconscious preference for certain letters of the alphabet over others.

7. Healers who use a technique called therapeutic touch claim to be able to manipulate what they call the "human energy field." They pass their hands over a patient's body, but don't actually touch the patient. Practitioners claim that patients who are ill have hot or cold spots in their energy fields. By massaging a person's field, they claim they can cure many ailments including colic in babies, symptoms of Alzheimer's disease, and even some types of cancer. Can practitioners of therapeutic touch actually detect a human energy field?

8. The ability to influence physical objects or events by thought alone is called telekinesis or psychokinesis. One extraordinary thing people with telekinetic power claim to be able to do is to influence the outcome of apparently random events. So, for example, by concentrating on a particular number, a person trained in telekinetic manipulation might influence the outcome of the throw of a pair of dice or the spin of a roulette wheel.

9. Graphologists claim to be able to discern a great deal about a person's character and personality simply by analyzing the person's handwriting. So, for example, if you don't care enough to go back and dot your i's, your handwriting shows that you tend not to pay attention to details. An illegible signature often indicates a desire to hide and escape notice. Similarly, claim many graphologists, a person who prints rather than writes may be trying to conceal their personality from others.

10. Everyone knows that Egyptian mummies have remained remarkably well preserved for thousands of years. The reason, claim some people, is that the mummies were entombed in pyramid shaped structures. In some way that is yet to be understood the pyramidal shape seems to focus a mysterious form of energy on objects housed within the pyramid. Advocates of pyramid power claim, for example, that organic matter of just about any sort can be preserved if it is housed under something with the shape of a pyramid.

11. *The following story appeared not long ago in major newspapers across the country. Comment on the design*

*of the experiment described, the results of the experiment, the attitude of the experimenters toward their experimental subject, and the extraordinary ability they tested. What is your conclusion? Is the last sentence of the story accurate?*

## SCIENTIST, ASTROLOGER TANGLE IN HOROSCOPE SHOWDOWN

*By Charles R. Tolbert*

One reason my family likes going to Chinese restaurants is for the fortune cookies. The fortunes get passed around, laughed at and commented on. Sometimes they are remarkably accurate, or at least that's our impression. I bet there are a lot of people who remember a fortune that was "right on." How is it they fit our personal situation so often when who gets which cookie is purely random?

Well, of course, the fortunes are written in such a general style that they can fit most anyone, but there is a more subtle effect: positive memory. With unusual events, we will always remember the remarkable coincidences and forget the times when nothing of note happened. This accounts for much of the "strange behavior" reported at full moon, for much of the "success" of astrologers and for the persistence of belief in palm readers. Because people remember the "hits" and forget all the "misses," such pseudo-science practices tend to get more credence than they deserve.

This effect is particularly difficult for scientists to deal with. When we debunk astrology, there will always be someone in the room that tells of all the times the astrologer has "read" them exactly right. No matter how logically we argue that astrology can't and doesn't work, it's hard to explain away positive, personal testimony. What we need are controlled experiments that can prove or disprove astrologers' claims.

Such experiments are hard to arrange because astrologers always say that the stars "impel," they don't "compel." In other words, astrologers don't generally make statements that are right or wrong, they make statements that are more or less likely to be true. It's hard to "make or break" a likelihood.

Luckily, we found an astrologer who was willing to make a testable claim. He said that given four horoscopes, only one of which was produced from a person's correct birth date and time, he would be able to identify the correct chart solely from that person's physical appearance. A colleague, Philip Ianna, and I decided to take him up on his claim and run an experiment to see how well he could do.

We arranged to collect the birth dates and times from a number of students in a large astronomy class. In order to insure that there was no error or collusion, we only used students who could provide a copy of their birth certificate. In addition, the astrologer claimed his method would only work on white Anglo-Saxons. Thus, no African-Americans, Hispanics, American Indians, or Jews were chosen. While he never made it clear why his method would fail in these cases, we nonetheless selected from the student volunteers only those who fit his criteria.

We were convinced from the beginning that if there was to be any useful conclusion drawn from our experiment, we had to carry it out under conditions that would be fully agreeable to the astrologer. Further, we made the experiment as "double blind" as we could. My colleague made all of the contacts with the astrologer, showed him the horoscopes, and was present for the meetings between the astrologer and the students. I, on the other hand, made all of the contacts with the students. I was the one who selected the student population to be used. I was the one who arranged for the correct horoscope and I was the only one who had the key to the correct birth dates.

After culling the students to fit the astrologer's criteria and adjusting for those who could not miss classes to meet the astrologer, we had exactly 28 students participating, split about evenly between men and women. We called in the students and had them meet, one by one, with the astrologer. He sat at a desk with the four horoscopes for that student in front of him. After looking at the students for a minute of two and hearing a few words from the student, he selected one of the horoscopes as the correct one. The letter (A through D) corresponding to that horoscope was placed on the list next to the number that represented the student.

This process was repeated for all 28 students, and then the astrologer's list was compared with the correct list that had been kept locked in my office. He got seven right - exactly the number that would have been predicted from pure chance. The astrologer could not explain why he had failed to do what he claimed to be able to do. Our conclusion was that his claims were bunk.

Based on what we can find out, the claims of astrology are all bunk but it is not often that science gets a chance to test them in so definite a way.[5]

## A SOLUTION TO EXERCISE 1

*(Note: Don't simply accept this solution. Satisfy yourself that the experiment is a good one! If you spot any problem, try to improve on the experimental design described below.)*

The explanation to be tested is that my doctor spends too much time talking with his clients about things having no obvious bearing on the problem for which the client is being seen. Keep in mind that we are not trying to establish whether or not my doctor "chats" too much with his clients. Rather, we are trying to determine whether extraneous "chatting" is the reason he falls behind schedule. We might test this explanation in the following way. First, we will need to obtain his cooperation. Suppose, then, we were to instruct him to consciously refrain from speaking with clients about things not directly related to the problem they are there to see him about. We might videotape

(with clients' permission of course) all of the appointments for a week. If the explanation at issue is right, we would predict that my doctor will, under these conditions, stay on schedule or, at any rate, come closer to staying on schedule.

This experiment seems to satisfy the falsifiability criterion. If chatting is the problem, it is hard to imagine any reason why he could not see more clients unless he is unable to follow our instructions. And we can check this out by reviewing the videotape. It is not clear, however, that our experiment will allow us to verify our explanation. The doctor's knowledge that he is taking part in an experiment may have some effect on the way in which he works. It seems possible that he will inadvertently work more quickly because he is nervous or simply aware that his work is being evaluated. If either possibility is the case, any improvement noted over the course of the experiment may be due to factors other than that for which we are testing.

Asking the doctor to work at a normal pace may just make things worse. However, we might take the precaution of taping a week's worth of appointments prior to giving the doctor his instructions. We can then use the first week's tape as a rough benchmark against which to judge whether he is performing at a normal rate during the week of the experiment. With this adjustment, our experiment does a better job of meeting the verifiability criterion.

## NOTES

1. From *Experiments in the Generation of Insects,* by Francisco Redi, translated from the 1688 Italian edition by Mab Bigelow. The Open Court Publishing Company, Chicago, 1909.

2. Paul Recer, "Satellite Supports Big Bang Theory," Jan. 8, 1993, *The Associated Press.*

3. William Harwood, "Discovery Offers Fresh Insight into Makeup of Universe,"

April 11, 2002, The LA Times-Washington Post Service.

4. *Test Your ESP,* ed., Martin Ebon (New York: Signet, 1970), pg. 73.

5. Tolbert, Charles R. "Scientist, Astrologer in Horoscope Showdown." *Oregonian,* July 2, 1992. Reprinted by permission of the author.

# 5

# Establishing Causal Links

## CAUSAL STUDIES

The search for causal explanations is of central importance in every area of scientific research. Often, the first step in understanding something involves speculating about what its cause or causes might be and then finding a way to test those speculations. In the last few years, for example, there has been a dramatic increase in the number of American children who are obese. What factors might be responsible for this increase? Too much fast food? Too little exercise? Some other factor? Some combination of factors? Causal experiments or, as they are usually called, causal studies are the main tool by which researchers confront such questions. As we shall soon see, designing and executing a study that can provide clear evidence of a causal link is a daunting task. In this chapter we will focus on the problems that confront causal researchers and at the ways these problems are typically solved in the process of designing, executing, and assessing the results of causal studies.

To get a feel for the sorts of problems causal researchers face, let's design a simple causal study along lines suggested in Chapter 4. Imagine that I've invented a new flea collar for dogs; it's made out of organically grown substances—herbs and the like—not synthesized chemical compounds. I call it the "Nature's Own Way" flea collar, or NOW for short, and I'm sure there is a market for NOW, given current concerns with the environment and the popularity of natural remedies. But one small question needs to be answered before putting the NOW collar on the market. Does it work? Will my new flea collar actually eliminate fleas? To answer these questions we might perform the following test.

First, we need subjects—a considerable number of dogs of all breeds, with a considerable number of fleas. So let's borrow, say, 500 experimental subjects from the local humane society. Next, we will hire a veterinarian and instruct her to screen our 500 subjects, eliminating all but the 200 with the most fleas. Then, by a random procedure we will divide the dogs into two groups. We will assign each dog a number, put the numbers in a hat and select at random two subgroups of 100 dogs each. After isolating the two groups from one another, we will board them in identical environments. Now comes the crucial step. We will put NOW collars on the subjects in the first group—the experimental group—but not on those in the second, control group. After two weeks, we will instruct our veterinarian to examine each dog for fleas.

Before we can undertake our study we must deal with three potential problems. The first concerns our prediction. Just what outcome should we expect to achieve? The problem is that most causal factors have a limited effect. If NOW collars are effective we will probably find some difference in the levels of flea infestation in our two groups. How big of a difference between the two groups is sufficient to establish that NOW collars prevent fleas? A second problem stems from the fact that most effects are not associated with a single causal factor. Even if NOW collars work, it may be that other factors have influenced the outcome in the experimental and control groups. For one thing, fleas may be more of a problem for some breeds of dog. How can we account for the potential effect of extraneous factors—like breed—in configuring our experimental and control groups? A final difficulty concerns the influence over the study exerted by experimenters and, in some cases, by experimental subjects. The veterinarian we have hired to inspect our subjects knows full well which ones are in each group. After all, only members of the experimental group are wearing NOW collars. Is it possible that her expectations will influence her judgment as she assesses the overall results?

Causal researchers must anticipate each of these three potential sources of difficulty as they design, execute, and assess the results of any causal study:

1. For most causal factors, the level of effect will be limited.

2. Most effects are not associated with a single causal factor.

3. Experimenter bias and experimental subject expectations may influence the outcome of a study.

Next, lets take a look at the techniques by which each of these problems can be addressed.

## LIMITED EFFECT LEVELS

We have all heard the claim that cigarette smoking causes lung cancer. However, this does not mean that all cigarette smokers will contract lung cancer nor even that all who smoke excessively for a long period of time will contract lung cancer. What extensive studies have shown is that more smokers than nonsmokers and more heavy smokers than light smokers will contract lung cancer. In an experiment designed to determine whether A causes B in C's, we would, thus, expect to find a difference in the level of B in the experimental and control groups. Ideally, it would be nice if we could predict in advance of our experiment precisely the level of difference we expect to get if there is a causal link between A and B. But this is not always possible. When the first studies of smoking and its effects were undertaken, researchers really had no clear idea of what the level of lung cancer in smokers might be. In part early research was designed just to determine this. However, we can say something in advance of an experiment about the level of difference required to establish that there is a causal link between A and B.

But first, we need to discuss a crucial procedure implicit in all causal research: taking samples from large populations. Consider again the claim: A causes B in C's. If C refers to some large populations, like, human beings or domestic dogs, our experimental and control groups will obviously contain only a minute fraction of the members of our population. Yet the conclusion drawn in a causal study is not to the effect that A does or does not cause B in the C's we have studied. Rather, the conclusion we will draw is that A does or does not cause B in C's generally. The reason is that we treat our two groups as samples from the larger population composed of all C's. So, for example, if a carefully controlled study were to show that 25 percent of the heavy smokers in the study contracted lung cancer, we would conclude that about 25 percent of all heavy smokers will contract lung cancer.

The "about" in the last sentence is crucial. Though a properly taken sample can provide us with some sense of what is the case in a larger population, such a sample will normally provide us with only a good approximation. A question we would naturally want to ask about the result above is: given that 25 percent of the sampled smokers contracted lung cancer, just how confident should we be that about 25 percent of all heavy smokers will contract lung cancer, and how much variance from 25 percent is close enough to constitute "about" 25 percent? The answer to this rather long winded question is: it depends. More precisely, it depends on the size of our sample. To see the connection between sample size and sample accuracy, consider a simple example.

Imagine we have before us a huge bag we know is filled with thousands of ping pong balls of two colors, red and blue. We also know that exactly half the balls are blue and half red. Suppose now that we take a random sample from the bag but a very small sample: we select two balls. What are the chances that the ratio of blue to red balls in our sample will match the ratio in the bag? Table 5.1, showing all of the possible results, tells us that in exactly half of our possible sampling outcomes (Rows 2 and 3), the ratio in our sample will match that in our population. Thus, we can say that if we actually took a sample of this size, chances are two in four, 50 percent, that our sample ratio will match exactly the ratio in the population.

## Table 5.1

| Selection | #1 | #2 | Row |
|---|---|---|---|
| | Ⓡ | Ⓡ | 1 |
| | Ⓡ | B | 2 |
| | B | Ⓡ | 3 |
| | B | B | 4 |

## Table 5.2

| Selection: | #1 | #2 | #3 | #4 | Row |
|---|---|---|---|---|---|
| | Ⓡ | Ⓡ | Ⓡ | Ⓡ | 1 |
| | Ⓡ | B | Ⓡ | Ⓡ | 2 |
| | B | Ⓡ | Ⓡ | Ⓡ | 3 |
| | B | B | Ⓡ | Ⓡ | 4 |
| | Ⓡ | Ⓡ | B | Ⓡ | 5 |
| | Ⓡ | B | B | Ⓡ | 6 |
| | B | Ⓡ | B | Ⓡ | 7 |
| | B | B | B | Ⓡ | 8 |
| | Ⓡ | Ⓡ | Ⓡ | B | 9 |
| | Ⓡ | B | Ⓡ | B | 10 |
| | B | Ⓡ | Ⓡ | B | 11 |
| | B | B | Ⓡ | B | 12 |
| | Ⓡ | Ⓡ | B | B | 13 |
| | Ⓡ | B | B | B | 14 |
| | B | Ⓡ | B | B | 15 |
| | B | B | B | B | 16 |

Now, lets expand our sample slightly. Table 5.2 shows the possible results for a sample of four. Note that in Table 5.2 we have four times as many rows as in Table 5.1. This is because we are now considering all possible outcomes from Table 5.1 when selection three is red, added to those from Table 5.1 when selection three is blue. (Rows 1–4 added to rows 5–8) This gives us eight rows and accounts for all possible outcomes for a sample of three balls. To account for selection four, we must double the number of rows for three selections. Thus, we must add Rows 9–16 to Rows 1–8, giving us a total of 16 rows. Rows 1–8 are all the results for three selections when the fourth selection is red: Rows 9–16 are the same three selection results when the fourth selection is blue.

But something rather curious has happened in our larger sample. First, the chance of getting a sample ratio that matches the ratio in the population has decreased. The ratio in our population, we know, is half red, half blue ping pong balls. But if we count the rows in Table 5.2 in which there are exactly two red and two blue balls, we find only six out of 16, or 37.5 percent, of the rows contain this ratio. (Rows 4, 6, 7, 10, 11, and 13) Remember, in our first sample—a sample of two—50 percent of the possible outcomes matched the ratio in the population. However, in our larger sample, something good has happened as well. Though our chances of getting the exact ratio have diminished, the chances of getting a sample ratio close to the ratio in the population have increased! Fourteen of our 16 rows contain either one, two or three red balls (rows 2–15) while only two rows (rows 1 and 16) contain none or four red balls. This, of course, is better than our first, smaller sample, where fully 50 percent of the possible outcomes contained all or no red balls.

These two samples illustrate an important point about what happens when sample size increases. As the sample grows in size, chances increase of getting a ratio in the sample that is very close to the ratio in the population. Our first, very small sample makes it look as though the chances of exactly matching the population ratio in the sample are greater in small samples. But this holds true only in those special cases where the population ratio matches a possible sample outcome. As we discovered, if the frequency of a characteristic in a population is 50 percent, we stand a one in two chance of matching the ratio in a sample consisting of two selections. However, consider what happens to our example if the ratio of blue to red balls in the population is, say, 73 percent to 27 percent. No sample of less than 100 can exactly match the population ratio! In general, then, the larger the sample, the greater our chances of getting a ratio close to that in the population; however, as sample size increases, chances of getting an exact match between sample and population frequencies decrease.

If, for example, we were to take a sample of 100 ping pong balls from our bag (once again, let's set the ratio of red to blue in our bag at half and half), we would find that fully 95 percent of all possible sample outcomes would contain between 40 and 60 red balls, though only about 8 percent of the possible outcomes would contain exactly 50 red balls. Similarly, if we were to take a sample of 1000 balls, 95 percent of our possible outcomes would contain between 470 and 530 red balls, though something less than 3 percent of the possible outcomes would contain exactly 500 red balls. Table 5.3 gives similar information for a number of sample sizes taken from a population, like our bag of ping pong balls, where the ratio of a given characteristic in the population is exactly 50 percent—that is, half the members of the population have the characteristic and half do not. So, for example, Table 5.3 tells us that if we were to randomly draw 500 balls from our bag, chances are 95 percent that our sample would contain somewhere between 230 and 270 red (or blue) ping pong balls. Our choice of the interval containing 95 percent of all possible outcomes is somewhat, thought not entirely, arbitrary. We could just as easily have settled on another interval, say, the interval containing 80 percent of all possible outcomes. Had we done so, we would have found it to be much narrower than the interval in Table 5.3., i.e., the interval containing 95 percent of all possible outcomes. In a sample of 100, for example, 80 percent of all possible outcomes fall between 43 and 57; for a sample of 1,000, between 480 and 520. Note that as we decrease the interval size, the range of outcomes under the interval also

**Table 5.3**

| Sample Size | Interval Containing 95% of all Possible Sample Outcomes |
|:-----------:|:------------------------------------------------------:|
| 25 | 7–18 |
| 50 | 18–32 |
| 100 | 40–60 |
| 250 | 110–140 |
| 500 | 230–270 |
| 1000 | 470–530 |
| 1500 | 720–780 |

diminishes, and for a pretty obvious reason: the interval containing 80 percent of all possible outcomes will have fewer members than the interval containing 95 percent. Our discussion of sampling has focused on the 95 percent interval because, as we shall see next, this is an interval used in much in scientific research.

Now, let's reverse our thinking a bit. Suppose that we have before us a huge bag of blue and red ping pong balls but that we do not know the ratio in the bag of blue to red balls. So, we take a sample from the bag, at random, of 1000 balls. We discover that exactly 500 of the balls are red, 500 blue. What Table 5.3 tells us is that we can be 95 percent sure that somewhere between 470 and 530 of the balls in the bag are red; had we taken 20 similar samples, we would expect 19 out of 20 of our sample results to fall somewhere between 470 and 530 red balls.

Consider finally a slightly different outcome to our sample. Suppose instead that only 400 balls from our sample turn out to be red. Table 5.3 is not going to help us a lot in figuring out what this ratio means, since it deals only with populations in which the ratio of the characteristic is half and half. Table 5.4, however, provides us with a helpful piece of information—the margin of error for various sample sizes. *Margin of error* is nothing more the interval in Table 5.3, expressed in percentage points, plus or minus, from the ratio in the population.

Table 5.4 gives us a easy but fairly accurate way of determining the reliability of sample outcomes like the one in the example with which we have been working. In a sample of 1,000 we found that 400 of the balls were red. In a sample of this size, the margin or error is roughly +/–3 percent. Thus, we can be 95 percent sure that somewhere between 370 and 430 per thousand, or 37 percent to 43 percent are red.

The information given in Table 5.4 can often be applied to media reports of polls and samples. Such reports are often sorely lacking in hard data. But by applying what we have learned so far, we can often draw some interesting conclusions on the basis of somewhat incomplete information. Were we, for example, to read of a poll in which the margin of error was reported to be "+/–4 percent," we could conclude that about 500 subjects must have been

**Table 5.4**

| Sample Size | Approximate Margin of Error* |
|---|---|
| 25 | +/–22 percent |
| 50 | +/–14 percent |
| 100 | +/–10 percent |
| 250 | +/–6 percent |
| 500 | +/–4 percent |
| 1000 | +/–3 percent |
| 1500 | +/–2 percent |

*The interval surrounding the actual sample outcome containing 95 percent of all possible sample outcomes.

polled. Sometimes reports of margin of error will mention "level of significance." This phrase simply refers to the percentage of sample or poll outcomes contained in the "+/−" interval. So, a poll based on the margins of error given in Table 5.4 will occasionally be reported as being "statistically significant at the .05 level." This is because, if 95 percent of all possible sample outcomes lie within the interval, only 5 percent, or ".05", lie outside the interval. Hence, in a poll of 500 subjects, reported to be "statistically significant at the .05 level," chances are only 5 percent that the population polled will vary by more than 4 percent from the poll results.

If a sample or poll relies on a smaller interval—say the interval containing 80 percent of all possible outcomes—the margin of error would have been smaller. But in such a poll, we could be only "80 percent sure" that the poll results reflect the proportion in the population on which the poll was based. Such a result would be reported as "statistically significant at the .20 level," since roughly 20 percent of all possible outcomes lie outside the interval with which we are working. Similarly, a result reported to be "statistically significant at the .01 level," would be based on an interval containing 99 percent of all possible outcomes.

Suppose, for example, that we were to read in the newspaper about a recent political poll. Fifty-eight percent of those polled reported that they were in favor of a ballot measure to be voted on in an upcoming election. The article also tells us that 500 voters were sampled. From these facts we can draw an interesting and useful conclusion. Following Table 5.4, we can conclude that there is a 95 percent chance, all things being equal, that somewhere between 54 percent and 62 percent of the electorate favor the measure in question. Remember, the margin of error for a sample of 500 is +/−4 percent. Had the report instead told us only that 58 percent of those sampled favored the measure and that the result is "statistically significant at the .05 level" or that the "margin or error for this poll is +/−4 percent," we could easily determine sample size. By consulting Table 5.4, we would find that the sample must have polled about 500 voters.

A note of caution is in order before we end our discussion of sampling procedures. When the percentages reported in a sample or poll are very high or very low, the intervals in Table 5.4 will be off a bit. The range of possible cases on the plus and minus side of the sample outcome will differ slightly from one another. But we need not be too concerned with this minor inaccuracy. The intervals in Table 5.4 are only approximate and are intended only to provide a rough estimate of the level of precision we can expect from samples or polls of various sizes. Unless sample results are very near to 0 percent or 100 percent, the intervals in Table 5.4 provide us with a fairly accurate approximation. Had, for example, our political poll revealed that 70 percent of our 500 sampled voters preferred the measure, the intervals would have been roughly the same.

Earlier, we raised a rather long-winded question. We were discussing a study in which it was claimed that 25 percent of the heavy cigarette smokers sampled contracted lung cancer. The question we asked of this sample was: given that 25 percent of the sample contracted lung cancer, just how confident should we be that about 25 percent of all heavy smokers will contract lung cancer, and how much variance from 25 percent is close enough to constitute "about" 25 percent? It should now be clear that we cannot answer this question without knowing the size of the sample. Let's assume 1,000 heavy smokers were involved in the study. After consulting Table 5.4, we could now venture the following answer: we can be 95 percent sure that somewhere between about 22 percent and 28 percent of all similarly heavy smokers in the general population will contract lung cancer. Put in a now familiar way, our interval is "statistically significant at the .05 level."

Now that we have a sense of how to estimate the accuracy of samples, we can return to our discussion of causal studies. Earlier we identified something of a problem. It is not always possible to predict in advance of an experiment the level of the effect we expect to obtain in our experimental group. However, as we noted, it should be possible to set some minimal difference in levels of effect between our experimental and control groups that would be sufficient to establish a causal link. We can do this by treating our two groups as samples and working with the margin of error for samples of the appropriate size. Our aim is to determine the amount of difference in the two groups that may be due to chance statistical fluctuations of the sort suggested by our discussion of margin of error. Only differences that have a high probability of being due to something other than chance statistical fluctuation will we regard as indicating a causal link. The minimal level of difference we will set, then, to establish a causal link, will be the minimal level that does not have a high probability of being due to sample error.

This will all make more sense if we run through an example. Imagine a causal experiment in which experimental and control groups each contain 100 subjects. At the conclusion of the experiment we find that 42 percent of the experimental group have the effect we are testing for while only 30 percent of the control group have the effect. Do we have evidence of a causal link? Look back to Table 5.4; the margin of error for a sample of 100 is approximately +/−10 percent. This tells us two things. First, since 95 percent of our possible

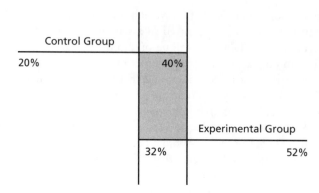

**FIGURE 5.1**

sample outcomes lie within this 20 percent interval, if we took similar samples 20 times, we would expect about 19 of our results to lie within this interval. Second, we can be relatively sure that the characteristic we have sampled for occurs in the population from which the sample is taken at a level somewhere within the 20 percent interval provided by our margin of error numbers.

But now we need to consider the relationship between the two samples corresponding to our experimental and control groups. In our experiment, 42 percent of the experimental group had the effect in question. This means that chances are good that in the general population exposed to the suspected causal factor, somewhere between 32 percent and 52 percent will actually have the effect. In the control group, somewhere between 30 percent, +/−10 percent—that is, between 20 percent and 40 percent—will have the effect. Figure 5.1 shows that there is considerable overlap between the two intervals.

Figure 5.1 tells us is that chances are quite high that the difference we have discovered is due to random statistical fluctuations in the sampling process. This result should not be taken to suggest that there is no link between the suspected causal agent and the effect we are testing. It is entirely possible that a causal link exists, but that the level of effect is too small to measure using groups of this particular size. What we can conclude, however, is that this particular experiment has not conclusively established such a link. Were the difference between level of effect in our two groups 20 percent or more, we would have concluded that the difference is due to something other than the random statistical fluctuations associated with sampling. Quite possibly, it is due to the suspected causal factor we are testing.

Had our two groups been larger, the same level of difference would have been significant. Suppose instead we had worked with experimental and control groups of 500 each. Table 5.4 tells us that the margin of error for samples of this size is +/−4 percent. Our intervals are represented in Figure 5.2.

Note there is a clear gap between the two intervals in Figure 5.2. We can conclude that the difference in levels of effect in our groups is in all likelihood due to the suspected causal agent.

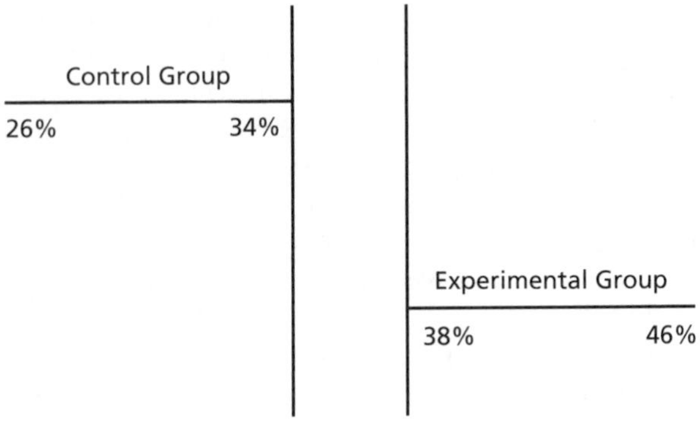

Control Group

26%                    34%

Experimental Group

38%                    46%

**FIGURE 5.2**

In the jargon of the causal researcher, failure to establish a causal link is often called a failure to reject the *null hypothesis.* The null hypothesis is simply the claim that there is no difference between levels of effect in the real populations from which the samples were taken. An experiment that succeeds in establishing a large enough difference in levels of effect between experimental and control groups will often be said to reject the null hypothesis. So, for example, in our experiment involving 200 subjects, our results do not enable us to reject the null hypothesis. But our larger experiment—our experiment involving 1,000 subjects—the null hypothesis can be rejected. And this means we have some evidence for a causal link.

Causal experiments do not always involve experimental and control groups of the same size. Even where the groups differ in size, we set minimal levels of difference in much the same way. Suppose, for example, that we have an experimental group of 50 subjects and a control group of 100. In constructing our intervals we need only make sure to work with the proper margins of error, which will be different in each case. Since we are working with percentages we should encounter no difficulty in comparing the intervals.

When the results of causal experiments are reported, researchers often speak of *differences* that are or are not *statistically significant.* Our earlier discussion of statistical significance can guide us in understanding this closely-related notion. A difference in the outcome of two samples will be statistically significant when there is no, or at any rate, very little overlap between the confidence intervals for the experimental and control groups. Thus, a difference that is statistically significant is one which is highly unlikely to be due to normal sample fluctuations; chances are slim that two groups, chosen at random, would accidentally differ by the amount we observed in our experiment. Conversely, a result that is not statistically significant suggests there is a great deal of overlap and that the observed difference in levels of effect may well be due to random sample fluctuations.

Reports of statistically significant differences should specify the confidence interval at which the difference is said to be significant. So, for example, a reported difference may be said to be "significant at the .05 level." This simply means there is a 95 percent chance the difference found in the two samples reflects a real difference in the populations from which they were taken. Similarly, a result that is "statistically significant at the .10 level" is one that stands a 90 percent chance of reflecting a real difference. Conversely, if we learn that a difference is "not statistically significant at the .05 level," we have found out there is a 95 percent chance that there is no real difference in the sampled populations. Whatever small difference occurred in the two samples is probably due to random statistical fluctuations.

More often than not, causal research uses the .05 level as a benchmark for statistical significance. When this is the case, Table 5.4 can help us to understand the results. But a note of caution is in order here. The intervals in Table 5.4 can give us a rough approximation of whether a difference in experimental and control group outcomes is significant. But they are a bit off. The percentage difference required to achieve "statistical significance at the .05 level" is a bit less than the difference specified in Table 5.4. For example, a difference of just over 13 percent will be statistically significant for groups of 100 or so. (The required differences decreases even more when levels of the effect are very near to 0 percent or 100 percent.) Table 5.4 suggests that a 20 percent difference would be required. The amount of overestimation in Table 5.4 decreases as the size of experimental and control groups increase. Table 5.4 suggests a 6 percent difference is required to achieve statistical significance for samples of about 1,000, when in fact just over a 4 percent difference will do the trick. We can correct for the inaccuracy in Table 5.4 if we adopt the following rules of thumb in working with reported differences between experimental and control groups:

1. If there is no overlap in the intervals for the two, the difference is statistically significant.

2. If there is some overlap in the intervals (if the intervals have less than one-third of their values in common), the difference is probably statistically significant.

3. If there is a good deal of overlap (more than one-third of all values), the difference is probably not statistically significant.

If we keep these points in mind, our method for setting levels of effect and of assessing experimental outcomes will serve us well.

In our discussion so far we have proceeded as though all one needs at one's disposal to design or assess the results of a causal experiment is a healthy sense of the logic involved in working with samples. But even the most precise and rigorous of statistical analyses fails to address another sort of problem with which we must contend. And this brings us to our second point about causes and effects.

## MULTIPLE CAUSAL FACTORS

As a veteran teacher with years and years of experience observing students, I'm convinced that students who attend class regularly generally do better on tests than do those who attend sporadically. But then personal observation can be misleading. Maybe I have just remembered those good test takers who always came to class since I would like to think my teaching makes some difference. Is there really a causal link between my teaching and the performance of my students? We can determine this by doing a test. I will teach two courses in the same subject next term, each containing 100 students. The only difference between the two courses will be that in the first, attendance will be mandatory, while in the second it will be voluntary. All material to be tested will be covered either in the textbook or in lecture notes to be supplied to all students. Course grades will be based on a single, comprehensive final exam given to all students in both courses. Suppose now that we have performed this experiment, and at the end of the term we discover a statistically significant difference between the test scores of the two groups. The experimental group, the group required to attend, scored much higher, on average, than the control group, most of whom, by the way, took advantage of the attendance policy and rarely attended class. To ensure accuracy we have excluded the five highest and lowest scores from each group, and the average difference remains statistically significant.

Despite the care we have taken in designing our experiment, it nonetheless suffers from a number of shortcomings. Perhaps the most obvious is the fact that it involves no control of factors other than attendance that might influence test scores. One such factor, obviously, is the amount each subject studies outside of class. Remember, tests were based solely on material available to all subjects. What if a much higher percentage of the subjects in the experimental group than the control group spent considerable time preparing for the final? If this is the case, we would expect the experimental group to do better on the final but for reasons having little to do with class attendance.

The way to avoid this sort of difficulty is by *matching* within the experimental and control groups for factors, other than the suspected cause, which may contribute to the level of the effect. Matching involves manipulating subjects in an attempt to ensure that all factors that may contribute to the effect are equally represented in the two groups. There are several ways of matching. One is simply to make sure that all other contributing factors are equally represented within both groups. This we might accomplish in our experiment by interviewing the students beforehand to determine the number of hours on average studied per week. Presuming we can find an accurate way of getting this information, we can then disqualify students from one or the other of our groups until we have equal percentages of good, average, and poor studiers in both groups. Another way of matching is to eliminate all subjects who exhibit a causal factor other than that for which we are testing. Suppose we were to discover that a few students in each group are repeating the course. We might want to remove them altogether from our study.

The final way to match is to include only subjects who exhibit other possible causal factors. We might do this by restricting our study to students, all of whom study roughly the same amount each week. If all of our experimental and control subjects have additional factors that contribute to the effect in question, the factor for which we are testing should increase the level of the effect in the experimental group, provided that it is actually a causal factor. Matching in this last way can be problematic if there is any chance that the effect may be caused by a combination of factors. Thus we may end up with an experiment which suggests that A cause B in C's when in point of fact, it is A in combination with some other factor which causes B in C's.

By matching within our two groups we can frequently account for causal factors other than the factor we are investigating. However, there is a way in which unwanted causal factors can creep into an experiment that matching will not prevent. We must be on guard against the possibility that our subjects will themselves determine whether they are experimental or control subjects. Imagine, for example, a student who has enrolled in the course that requires attendance but then hears from a friend about the course that does not require attendance. It seems at least likely that poor students will opt for the course that requires less. Thus, we may find that poor students have a better chance of ending up in the control section rather than in the experimental section. We could, of course, control for this possibility by making sure students do not know the attendance policy prior to enrolling and by allowing no movement from course to course. Another problem we might have here is that poor students in the experimental group, upon hearing of the attendance policy, might drop out, again leaving us with an experimental group not well matched to the control group. In any event, it is worth taking whatever precautions are possible in designing a causal experiment to insure that subjects do not influence the composition of the experimental and control groups.

## BIAS AND EXPECTATION

The biases of experimenters can have a decided effect on the outcome of a causal study. Also, when the experimental subjects are human beings, the expectations of the subjects can influence study results.

*Experimenter Bias* Think once again of our test of the role attendance plays in student success. Since I am the teacher, it seems only fair that I should be the one to grade the final exams. However, it seems a possibility that I will be a bit more lenient, inadvertently or otherwise, in grading the exams of the students in the experimental group. After all, I may have some vested interest in demonstrating my indispensability in the classroom. And if you think about it, my bias here may lead me to teach more effectively to the experimental group than to the control group; in teaching the former group I may spend more time with material that will be on the final exam. One way to avoid the possibility of this sort of bias on the part of experimenters is to insist that they do not know which subjects are in the experimental group or the control group. We might, thus, avoid the former problem, by mixing together all 200 final exams, prior to my grading them. The latter problem could be solved by having me videotape my class presentations rather than give them in person. Causal experi-

---

**QUICK REVIEW 5.1**   Questions to Raise in Evaluating the Design
or Results of a Causal Experiment

---

Has a way been found to control
for potential causal factors, other
than the factor under
investigation?

Is there any way experimenter bias
can influence the outcome?

Is there any way experimental
subject expectations can influence
the outcome?

Is any reported difference in levels
of effect statistically significant for
samples of the size involved in the
experiment?

---

ments in which the experimenter is unaware of which subjects are control and
which experimental are sometime called *single-blind* experiments.

*Experimental Subject Expectations* Psychologists have long known that an experimental subject's knowledge that he or she is taking part in an experiment can
influence that subject's performance. Psychologists call this the *Hawthorne
effect*.[1] For example, it is not hard to imagine, in our study of attendance and
test performance, that subjects in the experimental group might work harder
if they knew they were part of a group we expect to do well on the final exam.
The way to control for the Hawthorne effect, in this case, would be to make
sure students do not know they are taking part in an experiment, at least until
the experiment is over. Causal experiments in which subjects are either
unaware that they are part of an experiment or of whether they are members
of the experimental or control groups are another kind of single blind experiment. Experiments in which neither experimenter nor experimental subject
is aware of which subjects are members of the experimental and control groups
are called *double-blind* experiments.

Much medical research, for example, is double-blind. Experimental subjects
might be given a substance that is thought to prevent a particular condition.
Control subjects will often be given a placebo—an inert substance—to control for the possibility of suggestibility; experimenters who work with the subjects and who evaluate the results of the experiment, will not be told which
subjects are in which groups. The rationale for keeping the experimenter
"blind" is to control for the possibility that subjects may be treated differently
during the course of the experiment and to insure that the evaluation of the
subject's condition at the conclusion of the experiment will be unbiased.

## TYPES OF CAUSAL STUDY

So far in our discussion of causal studies, we have considered only examples
designed in the following way: we begin by selecting a number of subjects,
none of whom have the suspected causal agent, divide the subjects into two

groups, and administer the suspected causal agent to members of one of the two groups. Such experiments are called *randomized causal experiments.* But there are two other types of causal experiments, neither of which begin with randomly selected subjects who have not yet been exposed to the suspected causal factor: *prospective* and *retrospective causal experiments,* or as they are often called, causal studies. Prospective and retrospective studies typically provide less evidence of causal links than do randomized experiments, but in some situations, for reasons we will discuss in what follows, randomized experiments would be difficult if not impossible to undertake.

*Randomized Causal Studies* In a randomized causal study, as we have seen, subjects are selected and randomly divided into two groups prior to administering the suspected causal agent. Randomized studies are capable of providing strong evidence precisely because they enable us to control quite effectively for other possible causal factors. The fact that subjects were selected prior to being exposed to the suspected cause, coupled with the fact that they were randomly divided into experimental and control groups, both go a long way towards controlling for extraneous causal factors.

Randomized studies, however, have a number of disadvantages. They tend to be quite expensive and time-consuming to carry out, particularly if it is necessary to work with large groups of subjects. Unless the suspected effect follows reasonably immediately upon exposure to the casual agent, randomized studies may take a great deal of time to carry out. Does exercise have an influence on longevity? Though I suppose we might design a randomized test of the possible link between the two, the test would take years to complete. Finally, we would have grave reservations, to say the least, about carrying out randomized studies dealing with many suspected causal links. Do high rates of cholesterol in the blood cause heart disease? Imagine what a randomized experiment might involve. We might begin, for example, with a large number of small children. Having divided them at random into two groups, we will

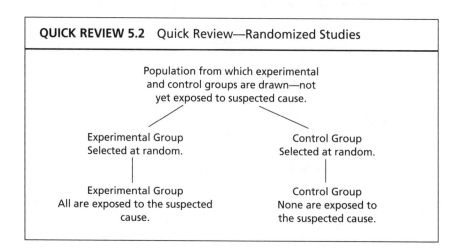

**QUICK REVIEW 5.2    Quick Review—Randomized Studies**

Population from which experimental
and control groups are drawn—not
yet exposed to suspected cause.

Experimental Group
Selected at random.

Control Group
Selected at random.

Experimental Group
All are exposed to the suspected
cause.

Control Group
None are exposed to
the suspected cause.

train one group to eat and drink lots of fatty, starchy, and generally unhealthy foods of the sort we suspect may be associated with high levels of cholesterol. I'm sure you can see the problem. Not coincidentally, much medical research is carried out on laboratory animals precisely because we tend to have much less hesitation about administering potentially hazardous substances to members of nonhuman species!

*Prospective Causal Studies* In prospective causal studies we begin with two groups of subjects, one of which—the experimental group—already has the suspected causal factor while the other group does not. During the course of the study, we wait to see any emerging level of difference of the effect in the two groups. Consider, for example, how we might carry out a prospective study to investigate the link between class attendance and test performance. We might begin by selecting a large number of students at random. Next we must find some way of accurately determining their patterns of class attendance. We might, for example, simply observe them for, say, the first ten weeks of my course. Next, we divide our subjects into two groups: those who attend class regularly (we might define "regularly" as those who miss less than 5 percent of all classes) and those who do not. The former become our experimental group and the latter our control group. If we find that more than half of our subjects are in one group or the other, we can pare down the size of the larger group by randomly excluding subjects from the larger group. Now, we track our subjects, and await the results of the final exam. Such studies are called prospective because they are future oriented. We select subjects who already have the suspected cause and wait to see what happens with respect to the effect.

To see the primary limitation of prospective studies, imagine that we actually carry out the study just described and discover a statistically significant difference in levels of test performance between the two groups; the experimental group scored much higher, on average, than the control group on the final. This result may not show us there is a link between attendance and test performance. In selecting individuals for membership in our experimental and control groups we were guided by a single consideration: class attendance. Yet there are clearly other factors which might influence test performance, one of which we discussed earlier: the amount one studies. Undoubtedly there are a number of other contributing factors such as how effectively one studies and how motivated one is to achieve outstanding grades and how much one already knows about the subject matter of the course. By concentrating on a single causal factor in our selection process, we leave open the possibility that whatever difference in levels of effect we observe in our two groups may be due to other factors. This, of course, is precisely where prospective studies differ from randomized studies. By randomly dividing subjects into experimental and control groups prior to administering the suspected cause, we greatly decrease the chances that other factors will account for differences in level of effect. In prospective studies it is always possible that other factors will come into play precisely because we begin with subjects already having the suspected cause.

Matching can be used to control for potentially troublesome causal factors in prospective studies. Suppose, for example, we discover that about 50 percent of our experimental subjects study five or more hours per week, per course, while only 35 percent of our control subjects study at this level. We can easily subtract some subjects from our experimental group or add some to the control group to achieve similar percentages of this obvious causal factor. It is not an oversimplification to say that the reliability of a prospective study is in direct proportion to the degree to which such matching is successful. Thus, in assessing the results of a prospective study, we need to know what factors have been controlled for via matching. In addition, it is always wise to be on the lookout for other factors that might influence the study's outcome, yet have not been controlled for. In general, a properly done prospective study can provide some strong indication of a causal link though, unfortunately, not as strong as that provided by a randomized study.

In some respects prospective studies offer advantages over randomized causal studies. For one thing, prospective studies require much less direct manipulation of experimental subjects, and thus tend to be easier and less expensive to carry out, and to occasion fewer ethical objections. Their principle advantage, however, lies in the fact that they enable us to work with very large groups. And as we have discovered, causal factors often result in differences in level of effect that are so small as to require large samples to detect. Moreover, greater size alone increases the chances that our samples will be representative with respect to other causal factors. This is crucial when an effect is associated with several causal factors. If a number of factors cause B in C's, we increase our chances of accurately representing the levels of these other factors

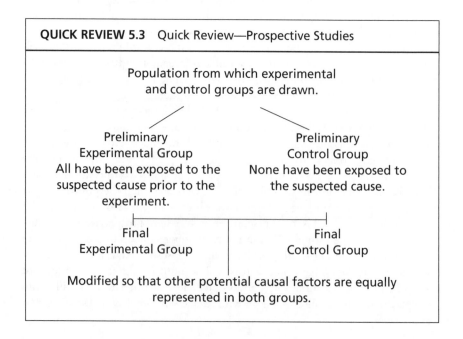

**QUICK REVIEW 5.3**   Quick Review—Prospective Studies

Population from which experimental
and control groups are drawn.

Preliminary
Experimental Group
All have been exposed to the
suspected cause prior to the
experiment.

Preliminary
Control Group
None have been exposed to
the suspected cause.

Final
Experimental Group

Final
Control Group

Modified so that other potential causal factors are equally
represented in both groups.

in our two groups as we increase their size. In addition, prospective studies allow us to study potential causal links we could not make the subject of randomized studies. As we pointed out earlier, we would all have serious reservations about a randomized study dealing with cholesterol and heart disease, in human beings at any rate. However, we should have no similar moral reservations about a study which involved nothing more than tracking people with preexisting high levels of cholesterol.

*Retrospective Causal Studies* Retrospective studies begin with two groups, our familiar experimental and control groups, but the two are composed of subjects who do and do not have the effect in question. Remember, in randomized and prospective studies, subjects will not have the effect being tested for prior to the beginning of the study. By contrast, retrospective studies look to the past in an attempt to discover differences in the level of potential causal factors.

To carry out a retrospective study of the link between class attendance and test performance we need only to look at records of past classes. We might begin by looking for students who have done well on my final, which we might define has having scored 85 percent or higher. We then select two groups of students: those who have scored 85 percent or higher and those who have scored lower than 85 percent. The former constitute our experimental group, and the latter our control group. Fortunately, I have kept detailed attendance records for all past classes. So we look at the attendance records for our two groups. If there is a link between attendance and test performance we would expect to find significantly better rates of attendance for students in our experimental group.

Even the best retrospective studies can provide only weak evidence for a causal link. This is because in retrospective studies, it is exceedingly difficult to control for other potential causal factors. Subjects are selected because they either do or do not have the effect in question, so potential causal factors other than that for which we are testing may automatically be built into our two groups. A kind of backwards matching is possible in retrospective studies. Suppose that in our study of the link between class attendance and test performance we discovered that 50 percent of our experimental group spent five hours or more per week preparing for each of their classes, while only 20 percent of our control group do so. It may be possible to do some matching here by eliminating subjects from one group or adding more to the other, and then looking to see if the difference in levels of the suspected cause in the two groups remains the same. However, even if by the process of backward matching we are able to configure our two groups so that they exhibit similar levels of other suspected causes, we have at most very tentative evidence for the causal link in question.

All we are in a position to conclude, as the result of a retrospective study, is that we have looked into the background of subjects who have a particular effect, and we have found that a suspected cause occurs more frequently than in subjects who do not have the effect in question. Whether the effect is due to the suspected cause is difficult to say even when pains are taken to control for other potential causal factors. For in manipulating other causal factors we may well have disturbed some combination of factors that is responsible for instances of the effect in our experimental group. That our two groups now appear to be alike with respect to other causal factors is, thus, largely because they are contrived to appear that way.

One final limitation of retrospective studies is that they provide us no way of estimating the level of difference of the effect being studied. The very design of retrospective studies insures that 100 percent of the experimental group but none of the control group will have the effect. Due to their limitations, retrospective studies are best regarded as a tool for uncovering potential causal links. We discover that a number of people have contracted effect B. Comparing them with a group of people who do not have B, we find a significant difference in the level of some factor, A. It would seem that A may well be a cause of B. To determine more here about the potential link between A and B, we would be well advised to undertake a more careful prospective or randomized study.

The advantages to retrospective studies, by contrast with randomized and prospective studies, are that they can be carried out quickly and inexpensively since they involve little more than careful analysis of data that is already available. And sometimes alacrity is of the essence. Imagine we have discovered that, say, Guernsey cows are dying at an alarming rate from unknown causes. What we need before we can do much of anything is some sense of what might be causing the problem. A quick search for factors in the background of infected cows which are absent at a significant level in the background of noninfected cows might turn up just the clue we need.

---

**QUICK REVIEW 5.4**    Quick Review—Retrospective Studies

Population from which experimental
and control groups are drawn.

Experimental Group                     Control Group
All exhibit the suspected        None exhibit the suspected
effect.                           effect.

Sometimes modified after all data is collected to equalize
the occurrence of other potential causal factors
in the two groups.

## READING BETWEEN THE LINES

The results of causal research are reported in specialized scientific journals. Typically an article will include full information about the design of the experiment, the results, and a complete statistical analysis where appropriate. (Many medical journals, like *The Journal of the American Medical Association* and *The New England Journal of Medicine,* also provide full disclosure of the funding sources of the research.) Conclusions will be carefully qualified and the article will probably contain suggestions for further research. When research uncovers a result which may have an impact on the general public it will often be reported in the popular media—in newspapers, magazines, and on television. And it is here—in the mass media—that most of us encounter the findings of causal research.

Unfortunately, the popular media tends to do a poor job of reporting on the results of causal research. Media reports will often leave out crucial information, no doubt, in the name of brevity; a 20- or 30-page journal article usually will be covered in a few paragraphs. Such reports tend also to dispatch with the kind of careful qualifications which normally accompany the original write-up of the results. For these reasons, it is important to learn to read between the lines of popular reports if we are to make sense of the research on which they are based.

Here, for example, is the complete text of a newspaper story about an important piece of causal research:

> Lithium, which is widely prescribed for manic-depressive disorders, may be the first biologically effective drug treatment for alcoholism, according to studies at St. Luke's Medical Center. The new evidence indicates that the drug appears to have the unique ability to act on the brain to suppress an alcoholic's craving for alcohol. The St. Luke's study involved 84 patients, ranging from 20 to 60 years of age, who had abused alcohol for an average of 17 years. Eighty-eight percent were male. Half the patients were given lithium while the other half took a placebo, a chemically inactive substance. Seventy-five percent of the alcoholics who regularly took their daily lithium pills did not touch a drop of liquor for up to a year and a half during the follow-up phase of the experiment. This abstinence rate is at least 50 percent higher than that achieved by the best alcohol treatment centers one to five years after treatment. Among the alcoholics who did not take their lithium regularly, only 35 percent were still abstinent at the end of 18 months. Among those who stopped taking the drug altogether, all had resumed drinking by the end of six months. (Researchers tested the level of lithium in the blood of the subjects to determine if they were taking the drug regularly.)

Just what are we to make of this story and the research it describes? Is lithium effective in the treatment of alcoholism? (Note that the story begins by claiming that lithium "may be" the first effective treatment for alcoholism.) In trying to make sense of an article like this one, it is necessary to try to answer a number of questions, all based on our findings in this chapter:

What is the causal hypothesis at issue?

What kind of causal experiment is undertaken?

What crucial facts and figures are missing from the report?

Given the information you have at your disposal, can you think of any major flaws in the design of the experiment?

Given the information available, what conclusion can be drawn about the causal hypothesis?

Let's consider again the news article about the lithium study, now in light of our five questions.

*What is the causal hypothesis at issue?* The hypothesis is that lithium suppresses the alcoholic's craving for alcohol.

*What kind of causal experiment is undertaken?* Randomized. Subjects are divided into experimental and control groups prior to the experiment and only the experimental subjects are exposed to the suspected causal agent.

*What crucial facts and figures are missing from the report?* The passage give us no information about what happened to the members of the control group. Nor does it tell us the number of subjects from the experimental group who "regularly took their daily lithium pills." We know that 75 percent of these subjects did so, but this could be as few as three out of four. All we are told of the remaining members of the experimental group is that 35 percent remained abstinent and that some stopped taking the drug altogether. We are not told how many are in each of these subgroups. It is possible that the majority of experimental subjects did not remain abstinent. Given the information we have at our disposal, we just cannot say for sure, one way or the other. Though we are given no information about the control group, we are provided with some information against which to assess the results in the experimental group: we are told that the 75 percent abstinence rate is "at least 50 percent higher than that achieved by the best alcohol treatment centers one to five years after treatment." However, we are not told whether the success rate for treatment centers is a percentage of people who entered treatment or people who completed treatment. If the former is the case, there is a strong possibility treatment centers have a higher rate of success than that established in the experiment. Once again, we can draw no conclusions since we are not provided with the key numbers.

*Given the information you have at your disposal, can you think of any major flaws in the design of the experiment?* One possible flaw comes to mind. It may be that the subjects who continued to take their medication (lithium or placebo) throughout the entire 18 months of the experiment were more strongly motivated to quit drinking than the other subjects. And this may have influenced the outcome of the experiment. Precautions need to be taken to ensure that either no subjects lacked this motivation or else that they were equally represented in experimental and control groups. Here, information about the results of the control group would be helpful. If roughly equal numbers of people dropped out of both groups, we would have some initial reason to think that we had controlled for motivation.

*Given the information available, what conclusion can be drawn about the causal hypothesis?* We can conclude very little, particularly because we are given no information about what happened to the control group. This is not to say that the experiment itself warrants no conclusion about the possible link between lithium and alcoholism. However the report about the study with which we have been working has presented us with so little information that we can draw no conclusion.

## SUMMARY

There are three types of causal studies:

*Randomized studies*—a group of subjects are divided at random into experimental and control groups and the suspected cause is administered to members of the experimental group only.

*Prospective studies*—subjects are selected for the experimental group who have already been exposed to the suspected causal agent; control subjects are selected who have not been exposed to the suspected cause.

*Retrospective studies*—a group of subjects are selected, all of whom have the effect. These subjects are compared to another group none of whom have the effect in an attempt to discover possible causal factors.

Of our various types of causal study, randomized studies provide the strongest evidence of a causal link. Retrospective studies provide the weakest evidence and are best regarded as a method of discovering possible causal links, not establishing them. In evaluating the design or the results of causal study, we must carefully consider each of the following:

1. Is the difference in levels of effect (or levels of cause in retrospective studies) statistically significant for samples of the size involved in the experiment? A difference is statistically significant if it is large enough to rule out the possibility of expected statistical variance in samples of the size being studied. In much causal research a difference must have no more than five percent chance of being due to such variance to be considered significant. To estimate how big this difference must be for samples of various sizes, review the discussion of interval estimation and overlap on page 84.

2. Have all potential causal factors, other than that under investigation, been accounted for via matching?

3. Can the possibility of experimenter bias be ruled out?

4. Can effects due to experimental subject expectations be ruled out?

5. Is the experiment clearly designed to provide evidence for a causal link and not just a correlation?

## EXERCISES

*Exercises 1–7 all involve applications of the statistical ideas presented in this chapter.*

*(On page 101 a solution is provided for problem 1.)*

1. In a study with experimental and control groups of 250 subjects each, the suspected effect was found in 45 percent of the experimental subjects but only 40 percent of the control subjects. Is the difference statistically significant at the .05 level?

2. In a study with experimental and control groups of 1,000 subjects each, similar results were found. Is this difference statistically significant at the .05 level?

3. In a study with 500 experimental and 1000 control subjects, similar results were found. Is the difference statistically significant at the .05 level?

4. A recent poll of 250 registered voters reveals that 45 percent prefer candidate X, 51 percent prefer candidate Y, and 4 percent are undecided. What conclusion can we draw about who is in the lead?

5. An even more recent poll of the same size shows that now 48 percent prefer candidate X, 49 percent prefer candidate Y, and only 3 percent are undecided. Can we conclude that the race is getting closer?

6. A brief newspaper story tells you of a randomized study involving small experimental and control groups. Though you are not told just how small they are, it seems reasonable to assume that they contain no more than 50 or so members. You are also told that the results of the study are not statistically significant. Can you draw any conclusions about the study based on this limited information?

7. Another story tells us of a large prospective study involving thousands of subjects in each group. You also learn that the results are not statistically significant. Can you draw any conclusions about the study based on what you know?

*Exercises 8–10 all involve applying statistical ideas we have discussed but in somewhat novel ways. (To solve 9 and 10 you may want to construct tables similar to Table 5.1 and 5.2.)*

8. I want to know how many trout are in my trout pond. I've taken a sample of 100 fish from the pond, tagged each fish, put them back in the pond, waited a while, and then have drawn another sample. 10 of the 100 fish from the sample have tags. Can you draw any conclusions about the number of trout in my pond?

9. If I flip a fair coin three times, what are the chances that I will

get all heads? All tails? One head and two tails?

10. A woman and a man, unrelated, each have two children. At least one of the woman's children is a boy and the man's oldest child is a boy. Are the chances that the woman has two boys identical to the chances that the man has two boys?

*Exercises 11–15 all propose causal links. Your job is to design studies of each of our three types—randomized, prospective and retrospective—for proposed causal link. As you go about designing each test, try to criticize your own work. In particular, make sure your are satisfied with the answers to the following questions:*

1. *Do you have a good sense, statistically speaking, of the level of effect required to indicate a causal link?*
2. *Have you controlled for other causal factors that might effect the outcome of your experiment?*
3. *Does your experimental design rule out the possibility of experimenter bias?*
4. *Does it rule out effects due to experimental subject expectations?*

*(On page 101 a solution is provided for problem 11. Look it over carefully before trying to solve the remaining problems.)*

11. Of all people who see chiropractors for lower back problems, 70 percent report some improvement within 90 days. Is chiropractic manipulation of the spine more effective at treating lower back problems than the methods of treatment employed by mainstream medical doctors? For lower back problems, medical doctors typically prescribe—antiinflammatory drugs and muscle relaxers and, in many cases, surgery.

12. Most states now have laws requiring the use of seatbelts by automobile drivers. By wearing seat belts, safety experts claim, we reduce the risk of serious injury or death in auto accidents.

13. Many dairy farmers claim that their cows produce more milk when they are listening to calm, soothing music, the sort of music we often hear in elevators and shopping malls.

14. Joggers, swimmers, cyclists, and tennis players are always bragging about the benefits of exercise. But are they right? If I exercise regularly, will I increase my chances of living any longer?

15. Clearly, a little encouragement helps us to do better in most things. Could the same be true for plants? If I think positive thoughts about, say, the geranium in my living room when I am tending it, will it do better than if I think negative thoughts?

*Exercises 16–30 present reports of causal studies from books, magazines, and newspapers, in short, from the very sources on which we base much of what we believe. For each passage, try to answer all of these questions:*

1. *What is the causal hypothesis at issue?*
2. *What kind of causal experiment is undertaken?*
3. *What crucial facts and figures are missing from the report?*
4. *Given the information you have at your disposal, can you think of any major flaws in the design of the experiment and any way of getting around these flaws?*
5. *Given the information available, what conclusion can be drawn about the causal hypothesis?*

*(Refer to the case analyzed on pg. 89
for an example of how to solve these
problems.)*

16.  A little exercise can help older
     people sleep better, researchers
     reported today in a new study.
     The study is being published on
     Wednesday in the Journal of the
     American Medical Association.

     The study, undertaken by
     researchers at Stanford Univer-
     sity, involved 43 sedentary,
     healthy adults, 50 to 76 years
     old, with mild to moderate sleep
     problems, like taking longer
     than 25 minutes to fall asleep,
     and averaging only six hours of
     sleep a night.

     Half of those in the study
     participated in 16 weeks of
     aerobics, with two hour-long
     low-impact classes and two 40-
     minute sessions of brisk walking
     or stationary cycling each week.
     The other half did nothing.

     At the end of the study, the
     subjects who exercised reported
     that they fell asleep about
     15 minutes faster and slept
     about 45 minutes longer than
     before. Those who did no exer-
     cise showed little or no
     improvement.

17.  Researchers have shown for the
     first time that non-smoking
     adults who grew up in house-
     holds with smokers have an
     increased risk of lung cancer.
     Although 83 percent of all lung
     cancer occurs among cigarette
     smokers, the researchers said
     their findings suggested that
     17 percent of the cases among
     nonsmokers result from second-
     hand tobacco smoke they
     breathed at home as children.

     The report was written by
     Dr. Dwight T. Janerich. Janer-
     ich's team studied 191 patients
     who had been diagnosed with
     lung cancer between 1982 and
     1984. The patients had either
     never smoked more than
     100 cigarettes or had smoked
     at one time but not more than
     100 cigarettes in the ten years
     before the diagnosis of cancer.

     The group was compared
     with an equal number of people
     without lung cancer who had
     never smoked. The researchers
     added up the number of years
     each person lived in a house
     during childhood and multi-
     plied it by the number of smok-
     ers to calculate smoker years.

     The researchers found that
     household exposure of 25 or
     more smoker years during
     childhood and adolescence
     doubled the risk of lung cancer.
     The risk of lung cancer did not
     appear to increase with house-
     hold exposure during adult life.

18.  In a study convincing enough to
     jolt any skeptic out of his ham-
     mock, investigators at the Insti-
     tute for Aerobics Research in
     Dallas have shown that even
     modest levels of fitness improve
     survival. Their work began with
     an objective measurement of
     fitness of 13,344 healthy men
     and women of all ages; it ended
     eight years later with a tally of
     those who were still alive and
     those who weren't.

     On entering the study, sub-
     jects were asked to keep up with
     a treadmill programmed to
     become progressively steeper
     and faster. Each then received a
     fitness score. By the end of the
     study, 283 subjects had died, and
     a disproportionate number of
     these had been in the least fit
     group. The least fit men died at
     3½ times the rate of the most fit

men. The disparity was even more marked for women—4½ times. Not only cardiovascular disease but cancer was seen more commonly in the least fit subjects.

Being above the bottom 20 percent in fitness level was a big advantage. Further improvement in fitness seemed to have little effect. Couch potatoes take heed: not much exercise is needed to improve the odds by a substantial margin. A brisk walk for half an hour a day will almost certainly suffice.

19. People who overuse a common kind of inhaled medication to relieve asthma attacks face a greatly increased risk of death, a study concludes. The researchers don't know whether the drugs, called beta agonists, are themselves to blame. But they said asthmatics nearly triple their chances of death with each canister of spray they use each month.

The research findings were based on insurance records from Saskatchewan, Canada. The study was financed by Boihringer-Ingelheim Pharmaceuticals, a German Drug Company. The researchers reviewed the records of 129 people who had fatal or nearly fatal asthma attacks. They were compared with 655 asthmatics who had never had life-threatening attacks.

The study found that fenoterol, a double-strength variety of beta agonist made by Boihringer-Ingelheim, was especially linked to complications. The risk of death increased fivefold with each canister of fenoterol. The study found that the risk of death

about doubled with each canister of another variety of beta agonist, called albuterol.

While use of the drugs was clearly associated with increased risk of death, the doctors could not say for sure that the medicines themselves were to blame. In a statement, Boihringer-Ingelheim noted that people who use beta agonists heavily are also likely to have especially severe asthma.

20. The question: should you be taking an aspirin every other day as a protection against heart attack? The answer: probably, if you are a man over 40.

The American Heart Association on Wednesday hailed new research that showed nearly a 50 percent reduced risk of heart attack in more than 10,000 men taking a 325 milligram buffered aspirin every other day. The physician's Health Study from Harvard University enrolled 22,071 male doctors in two groups. One group took aspirin; the other took a placebo. The researchers report, in this week's *New England Journal of Medicine,* that over four years, the doctors taking aspirin had 47 percent fewer heart attacks.

Among the 11,037 men who took an aspirin tablet every other day, 99 had nonfatal heart attacks while five had fatal heart attacks. In the placebo group of 11,034 men, there were 171 nonfatal heart attacks and 18 fatal heart attacks during the four years of the study.

21. In a dramatic and controversial finding, a team of psychologists has reported that left-handed people may live an average nine years less than right-handed

people. The study, which was based on an analysis of death certificates in two California counties, is the first to suggest that the well-documented susceptibility of left-handed people to a variety of behavioral and psychological disorders can have a substantial effect on life expectancy.

Halprin and Coren based their new study on 1,000 death certificates randomly selected from two counties in the San Bernardino area of California. In each case they contacted next of kin and asked which hand the deceased favored. All those who did not write, draw, and throw with their right hand were classified as lefties. Someone who wrote with the right hand and threw with the the left, for example, was counted as a lefty on the ground that many left-handed people were forced long ago to learn to write with the right hand.

The results shocked the researchers. The average death for the right-handed people in the sample was 75 years. For lefties it was 66. Among men, the average age of death was 72.3 for right-handed and 62.3 for left-handed people. "The effect was so large it is unlikely to have happened by chance," said Halprin.

22. (Note: *The following story appeared roughly two years after publication of the study that is the basis for exercise 21.*)

Being left-handed is not a hazard to your health after all, says a study that disputes an earlier report suggesting southpaws were at risk of dying up to 14 years sooner than righties.

Scientists at the National Institutes of Health and Harvard University examined the rates of death among elderly people in East Boston, Mass., and found that left-handed people were at no more risk than right-handed people.

Dr. Jack M. Guralnik of the National Institute of Aging, a part of the NIH, said the data came from a six-year community study that included 3,774 people 65 or older in East Boston. All deaths were recorded and analyzed.

Although the study was conducted for other reasons, Guralnik said, the information collected included whether the subjects were left-handed or right-handed. That enabled the researchers to test the theory that southpaws die younger than do right-handed people, he said.

"Over the six-year period, the death rate was 32.2 percent among right-handers and 33.8 percent for left-handers," not a statistically significant difference, Guralnik said. The preferred hand, or laterality, of the people was established by asking which hand was used to write and to cut with scissors. Those who used the right hand were considered right-handers. Those who used the left or either hand were considered left-handers.

Guralnik said 9.1 percent of the men and 5.8 percent of the women in the study were left-handed. He said the East Boston study was the most accurate way to find any differences in the rate of deaths between left-handers and right-handers because it compares population groups of the same age. Also, he said, laterality was established by direct interview with the subjects, not by—pardon the expression—secondhand information.

23. Weather might play a role in stroke, say researchers who pre-

sented the results of a 14-year study of 3,289 first time stroke patients last week at the American Academy of Neurology meeting in Denver. Dr. Dominique Minier said the researchers recorded weather conditions on the day of the stroke and five days prior. "There was a big decline in the number of strokes from an atheroma (a lipid deposited within the blood vessel wall, which thickens it and disrupts or reduces blood flow) in the large arteries during the warmer seasons," Minier said. "Further, we observed that there were a greater number of overall strokes and strokes caused by blockage of the large arteries in the brain and heart occurring when there had been a temperature drop five days previously."

24. In the mid-1970s a team of researchers in Great Britain conducted a rigorously designed large-scale experiment to test the effectiveness of a treatment program that represented "the sort of care which today might be provided by most specialized alcoholism clinics in the Western world."

   The subjects were one hundred men who had been referred for alcohol problems to a leading British outpatient program, the Alcoholism Family Clinic of Maudsley Hospital in London. The receiving psychiatrist confirmed that each of the subjects met the following criteria: he was properly referred for alcohol problems, was aged 20 to 65 and married, did not have any progressive or painful physical disease or brain damage or psychotic illness, and lived within a reasonable distance of the clinic (to allow for clinic visits and follow-up home visits by social workers). A statistical randomization procedure was used to divide the subjects into two groups comparable in the severity of their drinking and their occupational status.

   For subjects in one group (the "advice group"), the only formal therapeutic activity was one session between the drinker, his wife, and a psychiatrist. The psychiatrist told the couple that the husband was suffering from alcoholism and advised him to abstain from all drink. The psychiatrist also encouraged the couple to attempt to keep their marriage together. There was free-ranging discussion and advice about the personalities and particularities of the situation, but the couple was told that this one session was the only treatment the clinic would provide. They were told in sympathetic and constructive language that the "attainment of the stated goals lay in their hands and could not be taken over by others."

   Subjects in the second group (the "treatment group") were offered a year long program that began with a counseling session, an introduction to Alcoholics Anonymous, and prescriptions for drugs that would make alcohol unpalatable and drugs that would alleviate withdrawal suffering. Each drinker then met with a psychiatrist to work out a continuing outpatient treatment program, while a social worker made a similar plan with the drinker's wife. The ongoing counseling was focused on practical problems in the areas of alcohol abuse, marital relations, and other social or personal difficulties. Drinkers who did not respond well were offered in-patient admissions, with full access to the hospital's wide range of services.

Twelve months after the experiment began, both groups were assessed. No significant differences were found between the two groups. Furthermore, drinkers in the treatment group who stayed with it for the full period did not fare any better than those who dropped out. At the twelve month point, only eleven of the one hundred drinkers had become abstainers. Another dozen or so still drank but in sufficient moderation to be considered "acceptable" by both husband and wife. Such rates of improvement are not significantly better than those shown in studies of the spontaneous or natural improvement of chronic drinkers not in treatment.[2]

25. Women who took vitamins around the time they got pregnant were much less likely than other women to have babies with birth defects of the brain and spine, a comprehensive study has found. Anencephaly, the absence of major parts of the brain, usually is fatal after a few hours. Spina bifida, the incomplete closing of the bony casing around the spinal cord, typically causes mild to severe paralysis of the lower body. The defects are equally common and strike about 3,500 infants each year in the United States.

Researchers examined the data on all babies born with either of the two defects in the five-county Atlanta area from 1969 through 1980. The researchers interviewed mothers of 347 babies born with the defects and 2,829 mothers of defect-free babies chosen randomly for comparison.

The mothers were asked if they had taken vitamins at least three times a week during the three months before they became pregnant and at least three months after conception and if so, what kind of vitamins they took.

Fourteen percent of all the mothers reported taking multivitamins or their equivalent during the entire six-month period, and 40 percent overall reported no vitamin use whatsoever. The remainder of the mothers either took vitamins only part of the time or couldn't recall, the researchers said. Women who reported using multivitamins three months prior to conception and in the first three months after conception had a 50 to 60 percent reduction in risk of having a baby with anencephaly or spina bifida compared with women who reported not having used any vitamins in the same time period.

The researchers corrected statistically for differences in the ages of the mothers, their education levels, alcohol use, past unsuccessful pregnancies, spermicide use, smoking habits, and chronic illnesses. All of these factors have been linked to differences in birth defect rates in past research.

26. Women who use hot tubs or saunas during early pregnancy face up to triple the risk of bearing babies with spina bifida or brain defects, a large study has found.

A report on the study of 22,762 women was published in the *Journal of the American Medical Association*. Of the women studied, 1,254 reported hot tub use in early pregnancy and seven of them had babies with neural tube defects—errors in a tube-like structure of cells in the early embryo that eventually develops into the brain and spinal cord. That amounts to a rate of 5.6 defects per 1,000 women.

Sauna users numbered 367, of whom two had babies with defects, for a rate of 5.4 per 1,000 women. Fever sufferers totaled 1,865 women and seven bore babies with defects, for a rate of 3.8 per thousand.

Women with no significant prenatal heat exposure bore defective babies at a rate of 1.8 per thousand.

27. For the first time, a medical treatment has been shown to stop the development of congestive heart failure, a discovery that could benefit one million Americans, according to a major study released Monday.

Researchers found that a variety of drugs called ACE inhibitors can prevent—at least temporarily—the start of heart failure symptoms in people diagnosed with damaged hearts. The five-year study was conducted on 4,228 people at 83 hospitals in the United States, Canada, and Belgium. Half the people in the study took enalapril, one form of ACE inhibitor, while the rest took placebos. The study's findings included the following.

Among those getting the ACE inhibitors, 463 developed heart failure, compared with 638

in the comparison group. Taking ACE inhibitors reduced the heart attack rate by 23 percent.

There were 247 deaths from heart disease in those taking drugs and 282 deaths in the comparison group. This difference, though encouraging, was considered not quite large enough to be statistically meaningful.

The risk of being hospitalized was 36 percent lower in those persons taking the drug.

28. Men who were born small may be less likely to get married, at least in Finland. David Phillips of Southampton General Hospital in England and colleagues studied records of 3,577 men born in 1924 at Helsinki University Central Hospital in Finland. The 259 men who had never married were shorter, lighter, and thinner than the other men at age 15. The researchers wrote in a recent issue of the *British Medical Journal* that the factors that lead men to marry are complex, but "our data raise the possibility that early growth restriction influences the factors involved in partner selection, which may include socialization, sexuality, personality, and emotional response.

29. Running and other hard exercise may make many young women temporarily infertile, even though they may think they are able to get pregnant because their menstrual cycles seem completely normal, a new study suggests.

The researchers put young women on a two-month training program and found that only 14 percent of them had a completely normal menstrual cycle while they were working out. However, the irregularities could frequently be detected only by hormonal tests, meaning some women seemed outwardly to be having regular periods.

The research was conducted on 28 college women with normal menstrual cycles. None of them had ever been in physical training before. They spent eight weeks working out at a summer camp. They started out running four miles a day and gradually worked up to 10 miles daily. They also spent 3 1/2 hours a day in other moderately strenuous exercise, such as biking, tennis and volleyball.

Weight loss as well as exercise has been shown to disturb women's reproduction, so in this study, 12 of the women tried to maintain their weight while the rest went on a pound-a-week diet.

Only four of the 28 women had normal periods during the two-month program, and three of those were in the weight maintenance group. The researchers measured sex hormone production that is necessary for women to be fertile, and found abnormalities in the release of the hormones were extremely common during exercise, even when the women seemed to be having normal periods. If all had gone routinely, the women would have had 53 menstrual cycles during the exercise program. In 60 percent of these cycles, there were outward signs of problems, either abnormal bleeding or delayed periods. However, there were hormonal irregularities in 89 percent. Within six months

after the study was over, all of the women had resumed normal menstrual cycles.

30. Smoking more than a pack of cigarettes a day doubles the likelihood a person will develop cataracts, the clouding of the eye lenses that afflicts 3 million Americans, two new studies found.

The studies, involving almost 70,000 men and women, suggests about 20 percent of all cataract cases may be attributed to smoking, said a researcher who found a link between the eye disease and smoking in an earlier study. The latest studies involved 17,824 male U.S. physicians tracked from 1982 through 1987, and 50,828 women U.S. nurses tracked from 1980 through 1988.

In the Physician's Health Study, subjects who smoked 20 or more cigarettes a day were 2.05 times more likely to be diagnosed with a cataract than subjects who had never smoked, the researchers said. Of the 17,842 men, 1,188 smoked 20 or more cigarettes daily, and 59 cataracts developed among them, a rate of 2.5 cataracts per 100 eyes. Among the 9,045 men who had never smoked, 228 cataracts developed, a rate of about 1.3 cataracts per 100 eyes. Smokers of fewer than 20 cigarettes daily had no increased risk compared with non-smokers, the researchers said.

In the Nurses' Health Study, women who smoked 35 cigarettes or more daily, had 1.63 times the likelihood of undergoing cataract surgery as nonsmoking women. The number of nurses in each category was not given. Past smokers of more than 35 cigarettes a day had a similarly elevated risk, even 10 years after they had quit, the researchers found.

Unlike the doctor' study, the nurses' study showed a proportional increase in cataract risk with amount of cigarettes smoked.

## A SOLUTION TO EXERCISE 1

*The margin of error for samples of 250 is +/−6 percent. This means that there is a 95 percent chance that the level of effect in the target populations is somewhere between 34 percent and 46 percent for the population corresponding to the experimental group and between 39 percent and*

*51 percent for the control group population. There is enough overlap in the intervals to strongly suggest that the result is not statistically significant. Put another way, we do not have a large enough difference to reject the null hypothesis.*

## A SOLUTION TO EXERCISE 11

*(NOTE: Look the following solution over carefully. If you spot weaknesses in any of the proposed experiments, try to provide the necessary improvements. Pay particular attention to the various measures taken to control for extraneous factors. As a general rule, it is not a bad idea to ask others to comment on your solutions to the other problems. You may find that a fresh prospective will yield some interesting new ideas to incorporate in your experiments.)*

The causal link suggested in the problem is between chiropractic treatment (which is left unspecified but which generally involves manipulation of the spine) and lower back problems. The question we need to try to answer by our various types of studies is: is manipulation of the spine more effective at treating lower back problems than is treatment involving drugs and surgery? The passage does not give us the success rate of medical doctors in treating such problems, so we will want to design experiments that will provide us with information about the relative effectiveness of the two types of treatment.

1. *Randomized experiment.* We might begin with a group of people all having lower back problems of roughly the same severity and none of whom have yet sought medical aid of any sort. Where we might find such a group is difficult to say but we might cull a group of workers in a profession that is known to involve a high risk of back injury, say, furniture movers or longshoremen. Or we might simply run an ad in the newspaper asking for volunteers. At any rate, having found a group of experimental subjects, we will want to "fine tune" the group a bit to account for factors, other than treatment, known to influence the rate of improvement for back problems: weight, age, and fitness come to mind. Once we have come up with a group of subjects who are pretty much alike with respect to such factors, we will divide them into experimental and control groups.

Members of the experimental group will be sent to chiropractors for treatment and members of the control group will be sent to medical doctors who specialize in treatment of lower back problems. Since we know that 70 percent of people who see chiropractors report improvement within 90 days, we need to let our experiment run for at least that long. At the end of the specified period of time, we will evaluate the conditions of the subjects. If chiropractors are more effective than medical doctors we would expect more improvement in the experimental group.

1a. *Do you have a good sense, statistically speaking, of the level of effect required to indicate a causal link?* The level of difference in effect will depend, of course on the size of our experimental and control groups. If, say, we were to use two groups of 100, we would expect a difference in levels of effect of about 20 percent (or perhaps a few percent less) since the margin of error for groups of 100 is +/−10 percent. Any smaller difference would warrant the conclusion that the two types of treatment are approximately equal in effectiveness or that any difference in effectiveness is too small to measure in a study of this size.

1b. *Have you controlled for other factors that might affect the outcome of your experiment?* In selecting our initial group we took pains to ensure that all subjects had complaints of roughly the same severity and that all are roughly the same with respect to factors, other than those for which we are testing, that might contribute to improvement. One other factor comes to mind which might influence our results. There are no doubt differences in the effectiveness of treatment provided by various chiropractors and medical doctors. To control for this, we might want to specify the exact treatments each group will be allowed to use. Beyond this, it is hard to imagine what we might do to further ensure that we have really effective practitioners.

1c. *Does your experimental design rule out the possibility of experimenter bias?* One potential source of bias concerns the experimenter or experimenters who will be evaluating the results. It seems unlikely that most back problems will completely disappear after 90 days, so what will need to be assessed, in many cases, will be the level of improvement and one crucial measure of this will be the subjects' subjective reports of how much better they feel—how much less pain they are feeling and how much more mobile they seem to be. Assessing such reports will be difficult enough, since the reports may not be all that precise in any quantifiable way. Here, the preconceptions of the evaluators might influence their rating of various subjects. Hence it seems important that our evaluators not know whether subjects were members of the experimental or control groups.

1d. *Does it rule out effects due to experimental subject expectations?* This question raises a real difficulty for our experiment. We cannot hope to keep our subjects "blind" to the type of treatment they are receiving. And it seems possible that reports by subjects of their level of improvement may be tainted by their beliefs about conventional medical and chiropractic treatment. About the only thing we could do to control for this possibility would be interview our potential subjects prior to the experiment and eliminate those who seem to have a strong bias one way or the other.

One additional factor must be considered in our thinking about this experiment and what various results might be taken to show. As we noted earlier, we have as yet no information about the percent of clients who claim conventional medical treatment is successful for lower back problems. Nor, however, do we know the percent of cases in which such problems improve with no treatment whatsoever! Yet such information would be crucial to the proper assessment of our results. Suppose, for example, we were to discover that chiropractic patients improve at a significantly higher level than do the patients of medical doctors. If the level of improvement for those who seek no treatment is near that of chiropractors, we would need to consider two possibilities: first, that chiropractic treatment is not a causal factor and, second, that medical doctors actually do more harm than good. Fortunately, our results should provide us with some interesting information on this crucial issue.

2. *Prospective experiment.* In a prospective experiment we begin with two groups, one of which is composed of people with lower back problems who are seeking treatment by medical doctors; the other, our experimental group, will be made up of people with lower back problems who are being treated by chiropractors. Since our experiment needs only 90 days to run its course, we might admit only people who have started treatment within, say, 10 days, to insure that both groups will be treated over roughly the same amount of time.

2a. *Do you have a good sense, statistically speaking, of the level of effect required to indicate a causal link?* We may be able to work with larger groups than in our randomized experiment since we will only need to examine the records of existing patients, rather than recruiting a group of potential subjects who fall within a narrow set of guidelines. By beginning with groups much larger than in our randomized experiment, we will be able to accept a much smaller difference in levels of the effect as evidence for a causal link. If, for example, we could work with groups of 500, a difference of as little as 8 percent or a little less would suggest that one kind of treatment is more effective than the other.

2b. *Have you controlled for other factors that might affect the outcome of your experiment?* Many people seek chiropractic care only after conventional medical treatment has failed. Such people may well have problems that are, in many cases, much more difficult to treat than is the typical problem for which new back pain sufferers seek treatment. Hence, if a large number of chiropractic patients fall into this category, we would expect the success rate of chiropractors to be lower than that of medical doctors; a higher percentage of chiropractic patients will suffer from problems that have no quick and easy cure. We might control for this possibility by eliminating from both groups any subject who has been treated for their back problem by a medical doctor within, say, the last year or so. Another factor which may contribute to the success rates of the two types of practitioners, however, would be difficult to control. Our subjects have chosen the kind of treatment they are undergoing and it seems reasonable to suppose that many members of each group think the kind of treatment they are undergoing is the most effective; otherwise they would have selected the other type of treatment. (There are, of course, other reasons why people select chiropractors over doctors and vice versa; one reason why many people select chiropractors—even as their primary physicians—is that chiropractors are typically much less expensive than are medical doctors!) Perhaps we can do something about this problem by surveying our subjects and eliminating those with the most outspoken prejudices. A problem with this sort of "hands on" treatment of subjects, is that it becomes quite time consuming and expensive when dealing with the large groups that prospective studies have the potential to deliver. Other factors that may affect the outcome of our experiment—factors like weight, age, and exercise—can be controlled for by matching.

2c. *Does your experimental design rule out the possibility of experimenter bias?* The same precautions must be taken here as proposed for the randomized experiment discussed earlier. Our evaluators must be kept "blind" about whether subjects were members of the experimental or control group.

2d. *Does it rule out effects due to experimental subject expectations?* Our subjects have, in a sense, determined the group in which they are a member and their choice may well have been influenced by their beliefs about whether chiropractors are or are not more effective that medical doctors. Thus, we will want to make sure our subjects do not know the nature of the experiment when they are interviewed at the end of the 90-day test period. Otherwise, their evaluation of their own condition may be influenced by their attitudes toward the type of treatment they are receiving.

3. *Retrospective experiment.* In a retrospective experiment, we look into the background of subjects who do and do not have the suspected effect. It may seem that the appropriate study here would be one in which we look for differences in type of treatment for subjects who have reported success after treatment. However such a study does not meet the requirements for a retrospective experiment in that it involves nothing like a control group. So instead we might compare subjects who have reported improvement after treatment (the experimental group) with subjects who have reported no improvement after treatment (the control group). We can then look for differences in the percentages of people within the two groups who have been treated by chiropractors and medical doctors.

3a. *Do you have a good sense, statistically speaking, of the level of effect required to indicate a causal link?* In retrospective studies, there is no way of gauging the level of effect because all subjects in the experimental group will have the effect in question, while none in the control group will have the effect. We can, however, look for differences in the level of the suspected cause in the two groups. How we do so in this case is a bit tricky. Suppose, for example, we were to discover that among the experimental group, 50 percent were treated by medical doctors, 30 percent by chiropractors, and 20 percent by other kinds of practitioners. It may at this point be tempting to conclude that medical doctors have a better success rate. Here lies the value of our control group. Suppose among the control group, 70 percent were treated by medical doctors, 10 percent by chiropractors, and 20 percent by others. Suppose also that our two groups each numbered 1,000. Of the twelve hundred people from the two groups treated by medical doctors (50 percent of the experimental group plus 70 percent of the control group), 500, or about 40 percent, reported improvement; of the 400 treated by chiropractors, 75 percent reported improvement. This would suggest that chiropractors have a significantly higher success rate despite the fact that in our study the raw number of successful treatments for chiropractors is lower than that for medical doctors. Thus, it is important to have some sort of control group in order to assess the significance of the results obtained in the experimental group.

3b. *Have you controlled for other factors that might affect the outcome of your experiment?* We might attempt some backward matching. We might, for example, eliminate subjects who had a prior history of treatment if we found that more such subjects visited chiropractors. But such matching provides little additional evidence for any differences we might uncover since they are adjustments made after the experimental data is in, not prior to the experiment.

3c. *Does your experimental design rule out the possibility of experimenter bias?* The likelihood of experimenter bias seems low in that the experimenters will not have a chance to evaluate individual cases or to determine membership in the experimental or control groups. Attempts at backward matching might be suspect.

3d. *Does it rule out effects due to experimental subject expectations?* Though experimental subject expectations cannot influence the outcome of this experiment, something very similar does come into play. The initial decision as to which group a given subject falls into will be completely determined by the subject's own assessment of his or her amount of improvement. Moreover, experimental subjects' assessment of their own condition requires that they compare their current status to their recollection of their condition 90 days or so ago. Such comparisons are liable to involve a lot of guesswork and estimation and to be influenced by the subjects' beliefs about the efficacy of the type of treatment they have undergone.

# NOTES

1. The *Hawthorne effect* got its name from a series of experiments conducted at the Hawthorne plant of Western Electric Company in Illinois during the 1920s and 1930s. Researchers were interested in isolating factors that might increase productivity, factors like rest periods and lengthened and shortened work days. What they found was that just about any change seemed to increase productivity, leading them to conclude that the Hawthorne effect was in part responsible for the increases: the fact that the workers knew they were being observed led them to work more efficiently. Ironically, a reevaluation of the data from the original experiments many years later suggested the increased productivity of the workers at the Hawthorne plant was not due to the Hawthorne effect! Rather it was due to the fact that the workers had improved their job skills over the months during which the experiments took place. Though perhaps ill-named, the Hawthorne effect has been well documented in many other experimental settings.

2. Herbert Fingarette, *Heavy Drinking: The Myth of Alcoholism as Disease,* Copyright 1988. The Regents of the University of California.

# 6

# Fallacies in the Name of Science

## WHAT IS A FALLACY?

The faith of most people in the credibility of science is nearly unshakable. When we read in the newspaper or see on television that there is "scientific evidence for" or that "scientists have discovered" something new and interesting, our tendency is to assume that the evidence is impeccable. Certainly, the material we have covered in the previous chapters suggests that careful scientific investigation is perhaps the most powerful tool we have for getting at the truth of things. Unfortunately, the methods used by scientists to try to get at the truth of things can be, and as we shall see, often are misapplied.

In this chapter we will examine a number of fallacies committed in attempting to employ the methods introduced in the last four chapters. In logic, a fallacy is a mistake in reasoning. Thus, if I conclude that because (1) Morris is a mammal and (2) dolphins are mammals then (3) Morris must be a dolphin, I have committed a fallacy. The conclusion I have drawn, (3), does not follow from (1) and (2), even if (1) and (2) are true. Similarly, the fallacies we will examine in this chapter all involve drawing logically suspect conclusions in the process of applying some aspect of scientific method.

We must keep in mind here the difference between fallacious reasoning, on the one hand, and mistaken belief, on the other. Many ideas in the history of science have turned out to be mistaken, but the mistake they involve is rarely the product of fallacious reasoning. Prior to the mid-eighteenth century, for example, scientists believed in the existence of something called phlogiston, sometimes called the "fiery substance."[1] Phlogiston, it was thought, was the stuff responsible for a number of observable reactions in matter: among other things, it was thought to be the stuff released rapidly into the atmosphere during combustion, and slowly as metals decay. Now, as it turns out, there is no such thing as phlogiston; the scientists of the time were mistaken. However, the theory of phlogiston reactions was well supported by a large body of experimental evidence, indeed, the best evidence available at the time. Among other things, the formulae by which metals were produced from ores derived from phlogiston theory. Subsequent experimentation revealed a better explanation for reactions accounted for by pholgiston theory, one involving a new chemical element later to be identified as oxygen. The point to see here, is that both the work which established and ultimately overturned phlogiston theory involved correct applications of the methods we have been discussing. By contrast, a fallacy occurs when the methods of science are illicitly applied. Fallacious applications of the methods of science lead only to a false impression that something has been established with great care and rigor. Indeed, many of the fallacies we shall consider involve ways of lending the appearance of scientific evidence where there is little or none.

One well known fallacy in informal logic is called *argumentum ad hominen*—attacking the person rather than his or her argument. If, for example, I argue that every student ought to know something about science and, so, ought to read this book, you might reply that I receive a royalty from the sale of copies of the book. If your point is to mount an objection to my argument, you are guilty of an ad hominem fallacy. Even though what you say is true, the point you make is not relevant to the argument I have given. By pointing out that I stand to profit if students by this book, you attack my motives for arguing as I have, but you have not shown that my argument is flawed.

At the risk of committing an ad hominem fallacy, let me propose the following. Most, though certainly not all, of the fallacies we will discuss are committed typically by people on the fringes of science, not by mainstream scientists.[2] By "people on the fringes of science," I mean people who engage in fallacious scientific reasoning for either or both of two reasons. First, people commit fallacies because they have little knowledge of what rigorous scientific enquiry involves but nonetheless believe they are capable of undertaking such enquiry. Second, fallacies are committed by people who may well understand a great deal about science but who are trying to create the impression that there is some real measure of scientific evidence for something when in fact there is very little. Thus, errors of the sort we will discuss are sometimes committed inadvertently, sometimes intentionally. But no matter what the motives of their authors, such mistakes are instances of what is generally called *pseudoscience*. The distinction between genuine science and pseudoscience is one about which we will have more to say later in this chapter. But for now let's begin by taking a look at several common fallacies, all committed in the name science.

# FALSE ANOMALIES

Were we to do a quick search of an internet book store we would turn up a large number of entries on just about every extraordinary claim we have discussed in previous chapters. The literature on ESP, UFOs, ghosts, crop circles, alternative medical cures, and the like is nearly endless. A small sample of such books would quickly reveal a common theme. The author(s) would get our attention by laying out a series of apparently well documented anomalies and then in the body of the book go on to offer new and revolutionary suggestions as to what their explanation might be. All too often, however, the air of mystery surrounding the cases and events which have drawn us in will be no more than a carefully contrived illusion, as it were, a false anomaly.

One way to make something appear mysterious is to omit certain facts in describing the phenomenon, facts which suggest that the phenomenon may not be all that anomalous. In Chapter 2, we mentioned an apparent anomaly, crop circles. Large symmetrical geometric figures, circular and otherwise, mysteriously appeared in wheat and corn fields of Southern England and have since been observed in many other countries including the United States. We also noted that the circles are relatively easy to explain away given that there are tractor indentations near most of them and that several hoaxers have demonstrated how easily and quickly an intricate crop figure can be constructed. Yet most books on this phenomena conveniently omit these facts. Similarly, the six or so major works on the Bermuda Triangle, another example from Chapter 2, omit much well documented information suggesting that their favored anomalies are the result of accidents, inclement weather, inexperienced crews, and the like.

Another way to create a sense of mystery is to subtly distort the content of a factual description. For example, much research has been done in recent years on "near death experiences." Some researchers claim that people who have been near death, typically during a medical emergency, but who have been revived, have reported a remarkable experience. Here is an account of that experience from one of the best know books on the subject, *Life After Life*, by Raymond Moody:

> A man . . . begins to hear an uncomfortable noise, a loud ringing or buzzing, and at the same time feels himself moving very rapidly through a long dark tunnel. After this he suddenly finds himself outside of his own physical body, but still in the immediate physical environment, and he sees his body from a distance, as though he is a spectator . . . after a while, he collects himself and becomes more accustomed to his odd condition . . . soon other things begin to happen. He glimpses the spirits of relatives and friends who have already died, and a loving warm spirit of a kind he has never encountered before—a being of light—appears before him . . . at some point he finds himself approaching some sort of barrier or border, apparently representing the limit between earthly life and the next life. Yet he finds that he must go back to earth, that the time for death has not yet come.[3]

Now, if this precise experience were reported by many people, we would have quite a remarkable thing on our hands. In fact, the description provided in this passage is based on the reports of hundreds of people. But no two reports are precisely the same. The description we have just read combines elements from many varied experiences. Moreover, no single element in this description occurs in all reports and no single subject has given precisely this description. Though Moody quite openly admits all of this, many people who argue that near death experiences provide evidence of life after death, accept this artificial account as an accurate description of the strange experiences people report when near death. The fact that people are liable to report any of a number of things, that reports are frequently at odds with one another, and that many people when near death report no such experience, all suggest that there may be a more mundane explanation for the things people report when near death. At any rate the appearance of a great mystery here is exacerbated by the subtle fabrication of an experience that, strictly speaking, no one has ever had.

A final way to create the appearance of an anomaly is by overreliance on anecdotal evidence, a technique commonly found in works about revolutionary medical cures. For example, there are hundreds of books available on homeopathy, a type of medical practice discovered in the nineteenth century. According to homeopathic theory, a person can be cured of an ailment by being given minute doses of whatever substance creates its symptoms in a healthy person. Moreover, the smaller the dosage, the greater will be its effects. Precisely how and why homeopathy should work is unclear and is often chalked up to an "unknown mechanism." But does it work? The way to answer this question, of course, is to undertake a series of carefully controlled causal studies of the sort discussed in Chapter 5. Most of the books on homeopathy acknowledge that little rigorous scientific evidence is currently available. For a variety of reasons, few such studies have been done. Lack of funding and skepticism on the part of the mainstream medical community are often cited. Most authors make their case for the efficacy of homeopathy by citing numerous anecdotes—remarkable stories of actual people who have been cured by homeopathic remedies. Yet such anecdotal evidence is of little scientific value. It is estimated that about 50 to 60 percent of all the ailments for which people seek medical help will, if left untreated, go away within 90 days. Thus, the fact that someone has a problem, submits to homeopathic treatment, and gets better is not evidence that their improvement is due to the treatment! This crucial fact is always ignored as authors set forth their amazing stories of homeopathic cures.

A good piece of advice when confronted with evidence that is wholly anecdotal is to ask yourself, "What is missing, what haven't we been told?" A well known medium, John Edwards, claims to be able to communicate with dead relatives and friends of people in the audience for his television program, *Crossing Over.* On a typical episode Edwards will tell audience members things about their dead loved ones that he would have no way of knowing unless he were somehow in psychic contact with them. The program, of course, is carefully edited so that we are not privy to much of what he communicates that turns out to be wrong.

# QUESTIONABLE ARGUMENTS
# BY ELIMINATION

Suppose we know that either A or B must be true and subsequently discover that B is false. Logically we can conclude that A must be true. This pattern of reasoning is sometimes called *argument by elimination,* for it involves establishing one alternative, A, by eliminating the possibility of the other. An argument by elimination is fallacious when it ignores other likely possibilities in the process of arguing for one of the alternatives. Imagine that I want to establish a particular explanation. First, I list possible rival explanations and then proceed to show that none of the rivals is likely to be correct. Have I established my favored explanation? For two reasons, our answer here must be "no." First, there may be other possible explanations I have failed to consider. But, second, even if I succeed in ruling out all the rival candidates we can think of, the failure of these rival explanations only entitles us to conclude that the phenomenon in question needs explaining, not that my favored explanation is correct.

A common strategy in ESP research is to claim that an explanation involving some sort of extrasensory mechanism can be established by showing that experimental subjects can achieve results in an ESP experiment that would be highly unlikely by chance or luck alone. So, for example, a study might claim that a particular experimental subject has the gift of mental telepathy (the ability to read the mind of another) because he or she is able to guess the playing card an experimenter is thinking about more frequently than chance would suggest. Implicit in this claim is a fallacious argument by elimination. That the subject is telepathic follows only if we assume there are only two possibilities— either the subject did it by telepathy or by sheer luck—and can effectively rule out luck or chance under tightly controlled experimental conditions. Yet this assumption is flawed. First, there may be other possible explanations. Maybe an invisible imp peeks at the cards and whispers the right answer in the subject's ear. As wild as this "explanation" seems, it would appear to be as well supported by the experimental outcome as is the telepathy hypothesis. (What experimental outcome would support telepathy and rule out imps or vice versa?) Second, even in the absence of rival explanations, the outcome of this experiment does not confirm the claim that the subject has telepathy. The only conclusion we are warranted in drawing, based on the results of this experiment, is that something quite interesting, something we do not fully understand, is going on. What we are conspicuously not entitled to conclude is that we have evidence for any particular explanation.

# ILLICIT CAUSAL INFERENCES

People all too often draw conclusions about causal links based on evidence that is all too sketchy. In most cases, the inference of a causal link seems plausible only because rival explanations are overlooked or ignored. Conclusions about a causal link between A and B are often drawn on the basis of a number of specific kinds of evidence, none of which, taken alone, is sufficient to support a claim of a causal connection. The most prominent of these are:

1. A simple correlation between A and B.
2. A concomitant variation between A and B
3. The fact that A precedes B.

Let's look at an example of two of each and the plausible rival explanations our examples fail to take into consideration.

*A simple correlation between A and B.* In Chapter 3 we noted that the simplest sort of correlation is a claim about the levels of a characteristic is two groups, only one of which has another characteristic. Thus, A is correlated with B if more A's than non-A's have B. This does not necessarily mean that A and B are causally linked but people frequently make the illicit inference that they are.

Imagine we were to read the results of a study which purported to show a link between a person's astrological sign and his or her profession. Reading further, we discover that the birth dates of a large group of lawyers were examined and that it was discovered that more were born under the sign of Leo than under any other sign. Clearly, there is a positive correlation between being a lawyer and being a Leo. Now, this may suggest that there is a causal link between the two factors. However, there seem to be at least two plausible explanations for the data—explanations that do not involve any sort of causal link between profession and astrological sign. The first is that the correlation is just a *coincidence*. If we look at a number of groups by profession we may now and then find one where there is a significantly greater number of people born under a particular sign, particularly if we restrict our investigation to groups that are none too large. Imagine we were to do a study of plumbers and astrological sign. If we restrict our sample to a one or two dozen subjects, chances are quite high we will not find an even distribution under all signs. What we will find is some entirely expectable "clumping." Some signs will have more subjects than others. From here it is but a short step to a claim about a remarkable correlation between being born under a few astrological signs and becoming a plumber!

The fact that our study only cites one profession and one correlation, suggests another possible explanation. It may be that the researchers who undertook the study have presented us with only one small part of their overall data, the part that appears to confirm the possibility of a causal link. Or it may be that, convinced of the truth of astrology, they have inadvertently pruned away just enough data, say, by excluding certain subjects, to lend support to the idea of a correlation.

The explanation for a correlation need not be coincidence nor even fudging, inadvertent or otherwise. Frequently, correlations are explained by some third factor which suggests a possible indirect link between the correlated factors. Suppose, for example, that we discover from careful observation of a number of classes, that students who sit near the front of the classroom tend to achieve higher grades than do students who sit near the rear. It may be that this is a coincidence. At any rate it hardly seems likely that I can improve my grade simply by moving to the front of the classroom. What seems a more likely explanation is that students who want to do well are enthusiastic and want to sit "where the action is," namely near the front of the classroom. Thus, it may be that some additional motivational factor accounts for the correlation between the two factors in question.

*A concomitant variation between A and B.* Concomitant variation[4] is a convenient name for the second sort of correlation discussed in Chapter 3. Concomitant variation occurs when a variation in one factor, A, is accompanied by a variation in another factor, B. It is quite tempting to conclude that there must be some connection between A and B if changes in the level of one are regularly accompanied by changes in the level of the other. The problem with such a conclusion is that an enormous number of entirely unrelated things tend to vary in very regular sorts of ways. Over the past ten years there has been a dramatic increase in popularity of country and western music. At the same time there has been a corresponding increase in the cost of a loaf of bread. What is the explanation here? A genuinely baffling causal link? Some overlooked third factor? The most likely explanation is that we have managed to pick two completely unrelated trends that happen to be going in the same direction at the same time.

*The fact that A occurs prior to B.* In most circumstances, we would not automatically assume that because one event precedes another, the two are causally linked. But the inclination to infer a link increases dramatically when something out of the ordinary is preceded by something equally unusual. Our thinking seems to be that one remarkable thing must have an equally remarkable cause; if two remarkable things happen in close proximity, they must be connected. We have all had experiences like this before: just as you think of someone, the phone rings, and it is the person you were thinking about. ESP? Recently, an electrician fixed my furnace. A few days later, I noticed that the clock on the thermostat that controls the furnace was not working. It seems natural to conclude that something the electrician did caused the clock to stop. In such cases, the fact that one event precedes another is probably best explained as nothing more than a coincidence. What would be required to discount the possibility of coincidence, in the latter case, would be some sort of independent evidence linking the work of the electrician and the problem with the thermostat.

## UNSUPPORTED ANALOGIES
## AND SIMILARITIES

In attempting to explain something puzzling it is sometimes useful to consider something similar but whose explanation is well understood. Thus, for example, in the late nineteenth century, physicists hypothesized about the existence of what was then called the luminiferous ether, the medium in which light waves are propagated. They arrived at this notion by thinking of certain similarities between light and sound. Both appear to be wave phenomena and sound waves are propagated in a medium, our atmosphere, much as the waves created by dropping a pebble in a pond are propagated out of the surrounding water. Thus, physicists reasoned, there must exist a medium for the transmission of light waves as well, a luminiferous ether. Subsequent experimentation, however, demonstrated that there is no such stuff, and so physicists went on to consider other possible explanations for the propagation of light waves. Interestingly enough, physicists next thought about light in terms of another well-understood phenomena, electromagnetic fields.

This example illustrates the way in which thinking about a puzzle in terms of something similar but better understood can lead to possible explanations. But it also illustrates the need for independent testing of the explanation arrived at in this way. Analogies and similarities are fallaciously exploited when the fact that an explanation works in one case is given as evidence for the correctness of a similar explanation in another case. At the very most, a well chosen similarity guides us to a possible explanation; it should not be thought to provide evidence that the explanation is correct. Only careful testing can provide such evidence.

Consider one explanation often proposed by astrologers. Grant, for the moment, that there may be something to astrology and that, indeed, the position of the stars and planets at the time of our birth can influence our personalities or even our choices of profession. What is the explanation? How is it that the stars and planets influence our lives? Astrologers often give something like the following explanation:

> Much as the moon influences the tides and sun spot activity can disturb radio transmissions, so do the positions of the planets have an important influence on formation of the human personality. Modern science is constantly confirming the interconnectedness of all things. Is it any surprise that distant events, like the movement of the planets and the decisions people make, should be connected?

So the stars and planets affect our lives much in the way the moon influences the tides, etc. Of course, there is no claim here that the relation between stars and lives is precisely the same as between the moon and the tides or the sun and radio transmissions. What we have, then, is the barest suggestion that an explanation may be possible for astrological effects and that it may somehow be similar to whatever it is that explains the relation between moon and tides, sun and radio transmissions. What we do not have is any of the details of what that explanation might be. Nonetheless, by appealing to something that is understood, and suggesting the explanation for something else must be similar, our astrologer has managed to create the impression that something like an explanation has been given.

## UNTESTABLE EXPLANATIONS

To test an explanation we begin by devising a set of experimental conditions under which we predict that something will occur if the explanation is correct. If the predicted result fails to occur, we conclude that the explanation is probably wrong. What this means is that an explanation, to be subject to scientific testing, must in principle be falsifiable. Don't confuse falsifiability with falsehood. To be falsifiable is simply to be testable. By contrast, an unfalsifiable explanation would be one whose falsity could not be detected by any conceivable test. It may seem that an unfalsifiable explanation is simply true, but this is not so. An explanation that is in principle unfalsifiable is not a scientific explanation at all. Precisely why this should be so can best be explained by way of an example or two.

I cashed a large check yesterday and today discover that it bounced. Looking over my check register, I discover a glaring error in addition; I had much less money in my checking account than I thought. My miscalculation, then, explains why my check bounced. Had I not miscalculated, I would not have written a bad check. Imagine instead I gave this as the explanation for my bad check: "It must have been fate. What happens, happens." But what if my check had not bounced? Once again, fate, I say, is the real culprit. Now, it may be that fate determines what we do and do not do. But insofar as the notion of fate is consistent with everything that happens, it cannot be invoked to explain why a particular thing and not something else happened. Maybe fate determined I would bounce a check, maybe not. But by invoking the notion of fate I do not thereby explain why my check bounced as opposed to not bouncing.

A group of people, calling themselves "special creationists," claim that there is "scientific evidence" that the universe was created by God. Some believe creation occurred only a few thousand years ago while others believe it may have occurred billions of years in the past. Both groups claim however that the processes by which God created the world are "special" in the sense of no longer operating in the natural world; the "laws of nature" by which God created are different from those we currently observe. Well, this is all very interesting. But what prediction about the world could we make, provided this claim is true? The process by which God created so quickly and completely are no longer in existence so we should not expect to find evidence of their continuing operation. And for precisely the same reason we should expect to find no evidence against the theory of special creation. It would seem, then, that the creationist's explanation is consistent with everything that is happening or could conceivably happen, and so could not possibly be falsified.

But this means that the creationist account of how things began is not an explanation at all! To explain something is to try to make clear how or why it and not something else happened. A proposed explanation that is consistent with what happened and anything else that could have happened instead, explains nothing. Perhaps God created all things and did so in a very short time using special processes no longer in operation. But by venturing this scenario, the creationist has not explained why things are as they are and not some other way; the creationist's scenario is consistent with anything that could conceivably happen. Though the creationist's account is interesting, it is not a scientific account of things. Does this mean the creationist is wrong? No. What it does mean, however, is that special creationism does not constitute a scientific explanation.

If we find that an apparent explanation cannot be falsified, we have uncovered a compelling reason to reject it as an instance of genuine scientific explanation. It is always a good idea to ask of any proposed explanation: "Under what conditions would we be willing to set aside the explanation on the grounds that it is false?" If no such conditions can be imagined, we are dealing with something that is at best fascinating speculation, perhaps even an article of faith, but not a genuine scientific explanation.

Predictions made by psychics, tarot readers, astrologers and others claiming the extraordinary ability to foresee the future are often couched in terms that render them unfalsifiable. "A big career move awaits you," a psychic tells us. Just how big and just how soon we are not told. What would falsify this prediction? A few months pass and no new job is on the horizon. Is the prediction false? Well, the big career move may not involve a job change and whatever is to occur may still await us. As you can see, it would be hard to imagine anything that might prove false such a vague prediction. Astrologers are fond of cautioning their clients that the stars "impel, they don't compel." Presumably, what this means is that anything the astrologer predicts cannot be false since it may be about a future path the client will choose not to take.

Many conspiracy theories seem attractive and plausible largely because they are impervious to falsification. Imagine, for example, that I claim to understand why gasoline prices continue to rise at a much greater rate than the cost of living. There is, sorry to say, a plot, a conspiracy, among the major oil companies to insure that just enough gasoline is refined to keep demand slightly ahead of supply. Might I be wrong, you ask? After all, there have been many congressional investigations of the oil industry and none has yet turned up evidence for such a plot. Well what do you expect, I reply. The one thing we can be sure of in a conspiracy of this magnitude is that the conspirators are going to do everything necessary to cover their tracks, even if this requires buying the services of a few congressmen. Note here how I have attempted to turn the lack of any evidence against my theory into evidence that it is so. Thus, far from viewing its inability to be falsified as evidence that my theory is not scientific, I take this to be evidence that it must be correct.

## REDUNDANT PREDICTIONS

A common tactic of conspiracy theorists is to attempt to vindicate their theories by reference to the very facts that have occasioned them. You asked if my theory about the oil companies could be shown to be false. But you didn't ask for my evidence that it is true. That I am on the right track, I might contend, is shown by the fact that if there were such a conspiracy, we would expect gas prices to rise at an artificially high rate. And isn't this just what we find? The problem, of course, with my reply here is that I am using the very facts which have prompted me to give my conspiratorial explanation in an attempt to vindicate it. My thinking here is going in a circle since my prediction simply reiterates the facts I am trying to explain.

Much of the plausibility of many conspiracy theories stems from the fact that they seem to provide a simple and elegant explanation of a number of apparently unrelated but puzzling facts. So, for example, I might go a bit further and point out that it is because of the oil company conspiracy that we see not only the artificial rise in the price of oil but also that lobbyists represent the entire oil industry, not individual oil companies in the halls of Congress. Moreover, it explains why a few very influential congressmen accept large political donations from the oil industry and even why it is that we see so few independent gas stations today—gas stations not owned the major oil companies. Now, a whole series of rather interesting facts are explained by a single conspiracy. Yet in bringing in these additional facts, I am only showing that my theory can be extended to explain a lot. I have yet to provide any evidence that it is true. Though it no doubt sounds intriguing (who among us does not enjoy a good conspiracy?), my theory has yet to be supported by a single independent test.

No doubt there are conspiracies and conspirators, but their existence cannot be proven simply by spinning stories that would, if true, account for a myriad of interesting facts. One antidote to fallacious conspiracy theories involves considering the possibility of a discrete explanation for each of the facts the theory purportedly explains. It may be, for example, that the reason why congressmen accept large donations from the oil industry has little to do with the actual explanation of the demise of many independent gas stations.

As with conspiracy theories, we should be wary of any attempt to vindicate an explanation by treating known facts as though they were predictive consequences of the explanation. If I know that X, I cannot "predict" that X as a means of defending a particular explanation for X. One evening not too long ago, I passed a person I had never seen before just prior entering my unlocked office to pick up some tests that needed to be graded. But the tests were missing! My initial hunch was that the stranger took the tests from my office. Now, it may be that my hunch is right. But suppose someone were to doubt the correctness of my explanation. I do not provide independent evidence for my explanation by again citing the facts that have prompted my explanation, namely that I observed the stranger near my office, that the office was unlocked and that the papers were missing.

## AD HOC RESCUES

Explanations and claimed extraordinary abilities need not be dismissed simply because, in a given test, they appear to be false. As we found in Chapter 4, the test may have overlooked something that compromised the results. An initial test that fails to get the results expected can be modified and redone. But this sort of holding maneuver can only take us so far. If numerous modifications yield no different results, there is a point at which we must admit that our initial expectations were wrong. To persist in defending them after it is clear they are probably wrong is to engage in what is called an ad hoc rescue. To claim that some unknown factor must be confounding the test results is, thus, to make an ad hoc rescue.

There is nothing fallacious about rethinking and modifying an experiment when the results are inconsistent with expectations, particularly when those expectations have some measure of independent support. Such maneuvers are part and parcel of the way science is done. The discovery of the planet Neptune provides a good example. In the early 1800s, six of the seven known planets in our solar system seemed to obey laws set forth by Kepler and Newton. But the outermost planet, Uranus, traced out an orbit considerably different from that predicted by these laws. Why? One possibility was that the laws in question were a special case, capable only of explaining the motions of some of the planets. Another suggested a way for the laws in question to retain their generality: In the mid-1800s astronomers speculated that the peculiar movement of Uranus could be explained in a way consistent with Newton and Kepler if another planet outside the orbit of Uranus that was affecting its movement by gravitational attraction. Now, at this point in the story, we must regard the proposed new planet with a grain of salt. With no evidence for its existence, it seems suspiciously like an ad hoc rescue intended to save prevailing theory. Fortunately, however, astronomers were able to pinpoint just where the new planet should be in order to exert the postulated gravitational influence on Uranus, and shortly thereafter Neptune was discovered precisely where predicted.

By way of contrast, consider the following. Imagine that a psychic has agreed to be tested and further agrees that he can perform under the experimental conditions we have set up. Alas, our psychic fails the test. Nevertheless, claims our psychic, this does not show that he cannot do the things in question. For psychic abilities are subject to something called the "shyness effect"; psychic abilities ebb and flow and frequently seem to ebb just when we want them to flow. It is almost, adds our psychic, as though they don't want to be tested. It would seem that the psychic's appeal to the shyness effect is calculated not to help us rethink our experiment, particularly if there is no independent way of testing for its presence or absence. It is rather nothing more than an attempt to make sure that, no matter how carefully we design our experimental test, no conceivable result need be taken as repudiating the psychic's claimed ability. Unlike the planet Neptune, the "shyness effect" cannot be verified. Our psychic's maneuver seems clearly to constitute an ad hoc rescue. The only redeeming feature of the "shyness effect" is that, if true, it would save our psychic in the face of his failure to perform under controlled conditions.

# SCIENCE AND PSEUDOSCIENCE

Our long discussion of fallacious applications of scientific method provides a first clue as to how to distinguish genuine from pseudoscience. Genuine science involves the rigorous testing of new ideas; as such, the results of a genuine scientific investigation will employ the methods introduced in Chapter 2 through Chapter 5. Pseudoscientific ideas will frequently be supported by arguments and evidence that depend on one or more of the fallacies discussed in this chapter. Though adherence to the methods of science is at the heart of the distinction between genuine and pseudoscience, there are a number of other important differences between the two as well as a number of mistaken ideas about what the distinction involves.

*Science cannot be distinguished from pseudo-science on the basis of the quality of the results each produces.* In science, ideas earn their respectability not because they are right but, because they are developed and tested in the right sort of way. Many of the examples we have considered here and in preceding chapters serve to confirm this. At one point in the history of Western thought, the best informed scientific view was that the earth was at the center of the universe. Though this view was ultimately shown to be wrong, it nonetheless constituted the best science of the time. Though Ptolemy and his followers were mistaken, their view of the cosmos provided a coherent, testable explanation for a wide variety of phenomena. Our discussion earlier in this chapter of the luminiferous ether provided another striking example of genuine though ultimately mistaken science.

*The distinction between science and pseudoscience cannot be drawn along lines of scientific discipline.* We cannot say, for example, that astronomy is a science while astrology is not, that psychology is but psychic research isn't. This is not to say that astronomy or psychology does not deserve to be called a science. But the notion of a science, or scientific discipline, is much too broad for our purposes. My dictionary defines astronomy as "the science which treats of the heavenly bodies—stars, planets, satellites and comets", and I suppose this is as good a definition as any other. But within this broad discipline we sometimes encounter instances of pseudoscience as well as of genuine science.

For example, in the 1950s, a self proclaimed astronomer and archeologist, Immanuel Velikovsky, hypothesized that the planet Venus was created out of an enormous volcanic eruption on Jupiter. Velikovsky speculated that as the newly formed planet hurled toward the sun, it passed by the earth, causing several cataclysmic events, and eventually settled down to become the second planet in our solar system. Yet careful examination of Velikovsky's work has shown that the sort of cosmic ping-pong involved is quite impossible, and that Velikovsky either ignored or was unaware of certain physical constraints which his hypothesis violated. One of Velikovsky's most glaring mistakes involves a well-known law of motion: if one body exerts a force on a second body, then the second exerts a force that is equal in strength and opposite in direction. An explosion of sufficient magnitude to allow an object the size of Venus to overcome the gravitational attraction of Jupiter would simultaneously send Jupiter off in the opposite direction, despite Jupiter's great mass. Yet in Velikovsky's theory, the orbit of Jupiter remains unaffected by this most cataclysmic of events. Here, then, we have an example of pseudoscience yet one which we can certainly classify under the broad heading of astronomy.

Similarly, early in this century, the British psychologist, Sir Cyril Burt, claimed to have decisive evidence that heredity, not environment, plays the dominant role in determining intelligence. Yet as it turned out, much of Burt's work was based on fictional or distorted data. Burt apparently invented experimental subjects and altered test results to conform to his expectations in the process of trying to make his findings appear to be scientific.

*The distinction between science and pseudoscience has nothing to do with the distinction between "hard" and "soft" sciences.* The sciences that study human behavior—sociology, anthropology, psychology, political science, to name a few—are sometimes characterized as "soft" as opposed to the "hard" physical and biological sciences. Though in a number of respects the soft and hard sciences differ, none of the differences is sufficient to support the complaint occasionally leveled against the soft disciplines, that they are pseudosciences. The hard sciences do not have to deal with the complexities posed by the human ability to choose what to do in their attempts at describing and understanding nature. It is sometimes said that only the hard sciences are "exact" and this is generally taken to mean that predictions about human behavior cannot hope to be as precise as, say, predictions about what will happen to a gas under a specific set of conditions. Moreover, it is difficult to think of a single "soft" scientific theory that is as broad in scope as the theories of modern physics and chemistry. The law of gravity describes the behavior of all gravitating objects; it is hard to imagine a similar law describing a single aspect of the behavior of people, societies, economic, or political institutions.

Yet despite their obvious differences, the hard and soft sciences are all properly sciences. All aim at explaining phenomena of the natural world, be it the behavior of matter or the behavior of human beings. And both hard and soft sciences adhere to the methods we have discussed in Chapters 2 through 5 in advancing and testing their "hows" and "whys." Many philosophers argue that the social sciences will never produce the kinds of grand, unifying theories characteristic of the physical and biological sciences; it may be that the "soft" sciences will have to be satisfied with discrete bits of explanatory material, each of which is suited to a limited aspect of human behavior. But insofar as research in the social and behavioral sciences conforms to the more general methods of good scientific research, we have no reason to doubt their qualifications as disciplines capable of delivering genuine scientific results.

*Genuine science tends to be self correcting; pseudoscience is not.* We have examined a number of instances in which the results of scientific enquiry have been overturned. Yet in most cases, mistaken ideas have been rejected on the basis of further scientific enquiry. It is estimated that there are currently about 40,000 active scientific journals worldwide. These journals contain detailed synopses of research projects, generally written up by those who have done the research. An article reporting on new research will contain a description of the design and results of the experiment, discussion of the significance of the results and suggestions for future research. Most journals are "refereed": submitted articles will be reviewed by other scientists who will check to make sure the article is accurate and complete. The referees will finally decide whether the research described in the article is sufficiently interesting and important to merit publication. It is not unusual for a submitted manuscript to be returned to its author or authors for substantial revision. Thus, the process by which journals decide what to accept and reject serves to correct numerous potential errors.

This process is far from perfect. Given the sheer number of journals and articles, mistakes are bound to go unnoticed, some of them pretty spectacular. In the past few years, several instances have surfaced of published research that have involved fabricated data. Fortunately such incidents are fairly rare.[5] The fact that they have been discovered is itself a testimony to the self-correcting tendency of the process by which research is made public. When fraudulent research is detected it is usually by other scientists—peers who have taken the time to look carefully at the published results.

Scientific journals serve another function as well. They provide a forum for critics of current research. Often journals will publish articles aimed at mounting objections to and uncovering flaws in previously reported research. Since the early 1980s, for example, an enormous amount of research has been directed at understanding AIDS and its cause or causes. The vast majority of AIDS research points to a retrovirus—Human Immunodeficiency Virus (HIV)—as the cause of AIDS. This contention has emerged from thousands of experiments and clinical trials both on animals and humans undertaken by medical doctors, biologists, geneticists, and specialists in other related disciplines. Yet a handful of AIDS researchers, notably, Peter Duesberg, a professor of molecular and cell biology, and Robert Root-Bernstein, a professor of physiology, have mounted serious objections to the mainstream view. Duesberg argues that a careful analysis of the evidence strongly suggests that AIDS is not caused by HIV; Root-Bernstein believes that HIV is but one of several cofactors that must be present for AIDS to develop. Both have suggested that much of the research into AIDS and its causes undertaken in the last 20 years has been largely misdirected. As you might suspect, the work of Duesberg and Root-Bernstein has met with a great deal of resistance from the vast majority of AIDS researchers. In the last few years many articles have appeared in the scientific literature that are highly critical both of the methodology and findings of Duesberg and Root-Bernstein.[6]

This episode illustrates several of the reasons why science stands a good chance of correcting its own mistakes. Note first that the research criticized by Duesberg and Root-Bernstein was readily available in the form of published articles in scientific journals. Second, Duesberg and Root-Bernstein are themselves credentialed, mainstream researchers. Third, the critiques produced by Duesberg and Root-Bernstein were taken sufficiently seriously to be published in reputable scientific journals. Duesberg's work has appeared for example in both *Science* and *Nature,* two of the most visible and highly respected scientific journals. Finally, their criticisms were not simply dismissed out of hand, on the grounds that they were out of step with mainstream views. Other scientists have taken them sufficiently seriously to devote considerable time and space to rebuttals, again, in the forum provided by scientific publications.

Interestingly enough, most criticism of potentially pseudoscientific research comes from within mainstream science as well. Recent criticism, for example, of the work of the special creationists, has been leveled by mainstream anthropologists, zoologists, biologists, and evolutionary theorists. Though there are a small number of journals devoted to creationist science, it is rare to find a single article by a noted creationist critical of the work of other creationists.

*As a scientific discipline develops it will gradually produce a maturing body of explanatory or theoretical findings; pseudoscience produces very little theory.* One major aim of science, as we discussed in Chapter 1, is to "make sense" of nature by providing better and better and, often, more and more encompassing bodies of explanatory material. Think, for example, of all that is known about the mechanisms involved in the transmission of genetic information from one generation to the next, by contrast with what was known 150 years ago at the birth of the science of genetics. Gregor Mendel, the founder of genetic research, introduced the somewhat vague and mysterious notion of a "genetic factor" in his attempts to explain the observable characteristics of some simple varieties of plants. Today, modern geneticists can provide us with the details of the explanation Mendel could only hint at—an explanation involving the ways in which instructions encoded in DNA (a notion wholly unknown to Mendel) are responsible for those characteristics.

By contrast, pseudoscientific research almost always produces spectacular claims for extraordinary abilities and events, but little else. Ideas tend not to develop and mature over time as they do in genuine science. As it turns out, ESP research began only a little later than did genetic research. Yet today we find little more than an enormous body of controversial evidence that a few people have psychic ability and almost no theoretical understanding of how ESP might work. What little explanatory material emerges in many pseudoscientific endeavors is likely to be based on vague analogies and similarities drawn from some well understood area of science. So, for example, a book on ESP published in the 1930s was entitled, *ESP: Mental Radio.* An interesting idea, but hardly a reliable explanation.

*The findings, theoretical and otherwise, of genuine science are always open to revision; rarely do pseudo-scientific claims change much over time.* It is hard to imagine a thriving scientific discipline today wherein much of what was believed 100 or even 50 years ago has not been supplanted by a more accurate picture of things. Fifty years ago, particle physics provided us with a picture of the world in which the most fundamental particles were the electron, proton, and neutron. A few stray experimental results were in conflict with this picture, but few physicists questioned its rough fit with reality. Today physics provides a more comprehensive picture in which protons and neutrons are composites built out of more fundamental particles, quarks. The landscape of the particle physicists has change dramatically in a brief period of time. The openness of science to revision does not mean that scientific results cannot achieve a kind of permanence. Many of the findings of science will doubtless not be repudiated by new research. Science will not discover that water molecules are composed of something other than two atoms of hydrogen and one of oxygen; no one doubts that Newton was correct in seeing that gravitational attraction is directly proportional to mass and inversely proportional to distance. The changes we can anticipate in well established areas of science will generally occur at the level of underlying explanation. Why do gravitating objects behave in the way Newton discovered? What is the internal structure of the "stuff" of water? And just how if at all are the forces at work inside the atom connected to the force responsible for gravity?

By way of contrast, it is interesting to look at the work of modern astrologers. If you were to have a competent astrologer draw a detailed horoscope, his or her work would be based on classic astrological texts, written nearly 2,000 years ago. Pseudoscientists often claim the long history of their ideas to be evidence for their correctness. Thus, an astrologer might boast that his or her techniques are derived from the discoveries of ancient Babylonian and Egyptian astronomers. In and of itself, this is not reason to classify astrology as a pseudoscience. But at the level of underlying explanation, astrology remains today in much the position it was at its inception. After 2,000 years astrologers have conspicuously failed to produce even the beginnings of a plausible explanation for its purported effects. Conspicuously missing in the history of astrological research is any evidence of the kind of proposing, testing, modifying, and revising of new ideas that typifies scientific progress.

*Genuine science embraces skepticism; pseudoscience tends to view skepticism as a sign of narrow-mindedness.* The first reaction of a competent scientist, when faced with something new and unusual, is to try to explain the phenomena away by fitting it into what is already known. Many people who engage in pseudoscience see this as the worst sort of skepticism; the fact that one's initial reaction is to try to rob something of its mystery is taken to be a sign that one is unwilling to entertain new ideas. It is perhaps this attitude toward scientific skepticism more than anything else that contributes to the tendency in pseudoscience to accept claims in the absence of solid scientific evidence.

The question of whether a piece of "scientific" research is genuine or bogus is not always easy to answer. Though the points we have discussed in this section can provide us with some initial sense of when we are in the presence of pseudoscience, we should not apply them dogmatically. If someone purports to have "scientific evidence" for something, we should not dismiss their work simply because, for example, they refuse to countenance serious criticism, complain that their critics lack an open mind, or proclaim the longevity of their ideas. Rather, such moves should only be taken as a sign that something may well be seriously amiss. The fundamental difference between science, genuine and bogus, is really a difference in method. The results of genuine scientific enquiry are the product of open and honest applications of the methods we have discussed in previous chapters. Pseudoscientific results, by contrast, are produced with little regard for these methods.

A person claims to have "scientific evidence" for X. Are we confronted with genuine science or pseudoscience? To answer this question there is no substitute for taking a careful, critical look at the methods employed in establishing and explaining X.

## THE LIMITS OF SCIENTIFIC EXPLANATION

In Chapter 1 we said that one major goal of science is to further our understanding of how and why things happen as they do. One issue deserves some brief discussion before we conclude: are there hows and whys that science cannot help to answer? Are there things, that is, that science is powerless to explain?

With respect to questions about processes occurring in the natural world, it is hard to imagine a limit to the potential of science to explain. This does not mean that science, given enough time and effort, will provide us with an understanding of all natural processes. What it does mean is that there appears to be no limits to the questions—questions about the natural world—which science, properly carried out, cannot profitably address. And if it turns out that there are such limits, we will discover them only by approaching them scientifically and discovering just how far this approach can carry us.

But there other hows and other whys—that take us beyond the interests we normally associate with scientific enquiry. These are the great questions of metaphysics, questions that have vexed philosophers and ordinary people alike for as long as people have thought. They are questions you have probably wondered about in some idle moment: Why is there anything at all, rather than nothing? Is there some benevolent, creative force responsible for the natural world? Is there, in other words, a God? Why are we here? Do our lives have some ultimate meaning, some cosmic purpose?

Deep metaphysical questions like these, I suspect, will not be settled by scientific enquiry. This is not to suggest that science is somehow deficient. The methods of science are not designed to answer questions of this sort. Science aims to explain processes occurring within the natural world; by contrast, deep metaphysical questions like those above raise issues about the nature of the natural world itself. They are not concerned with mechanisms, causes, laws, the very stuff of scientific explanation. They involve, rather, an attempt to understand the purposes behind the sum total of the natural world. If scientific questions are, by definition, questions about how and why things happen in the natural world, then metaphysical questions are by definition not scientific questions. Even if science were somehow, someday to provide us with an utterly complete explanatory picture of all processes in nature—a theory of everything—science would leave our deep metaphysical questions untouched. Why this particular set of explanations and not another? What is their cosmic significance? Their purpose? Who is their author?

Not long before his death, Sir Peter Medawar, Noble laureate in medicine, made the following observation. "Catastrophe apart, I believe it to be science's greatest glory that there is no limit upon the power of science to answer questions of the kind science can answer."[7] Metaphysical questions aside, there would seem to be no limit upon the ability of science to explain so long as we restrict science to the kind of question, as Medawar says, science can answer.

## SUMMARY

Here is a brief summary of the fallacies we have discussed and of the tell-tale signs of a pseudoscience.

*Fallacies Committed in the Name of Science*

*False Anomalies:* Creating the impression that something is anomalous by distorting or omitting facts that suggests a nonanomalous explanation or by overreliance on anecdotal evidence.

*Questionable Arguments by Elimination:* Arguing against rival explanations rather than providing evidence for a given explanation.

*Illicit Causal Inferences:* Inferring a causal link on the basis of a correlation, concomitant variation, or the fact that the suspected cause occurred before its effect. Possible rival explanations are: coincidence, fudging of data, and third factors.

*Unsupported Analogies and Similarities:* Defending a novel, untested explanation by implying that it is similar to another, well supported explanation.

*Untestable Explanations:* Advancing an explanatory claim that is consistent with everything that could happen or offering a prediction that cannot be falsified.

*Redundant Predictions:* Treating the observations that have occasioned an explanation as evidence confirming the explanation.

*Ad Hoc Rescues:* Advancing untestable excuses as a means of saving an otherwise discredited explanation or extraordinary claim.

*The Telltale Signs of Pseudoscience*

Pseudoscientific claims often involve fallacious scientific reasoning of the sort exemplified by the fallacies above.

Pseudoscience can occur within the bounds of legitimate scientific disciplines.

Pseudoscience tends not to be self-correcting.

Pseudoscience produces very little explanatory theory.

Rarely do pseudoscientific claims change much over time; pseudoscientists take this fact to be a scientific virtue.

Pseudoscientists tend to view skepticism as a sign of narrow-mindedness.

## EXERCISES

*Many of the following passages involve one or more of the fallacies we have discussed. Comment on any fallacies you find; name them and explain in more detail how each involves the fallacy or fallacies you have uncovered. When appropriate, speculate about rival explanations that are overlooked. Be on the lookout for examples of the other characteristic features of pseudoscience and comment on any you find. Problems you will encounter in some of the passages will be difficult to classify and in thinking about mistakes they may involve, you will need to rely on your by now well developed sense of what good scientific research involves. In other words, you may need to apply some of the ideas presented in Chapters 2 through 5.*

(Note: A solution to Exercise 1 is provided on page 135.)

1.  A remarkable fact is that many of the great scientists and mathematicians in history have had a deep interest in music. Einstein, for example, was a devoted amateur violinist and Newton is said to have been fascinated by the mathematical structure of musical compositions. If you want your child to pursue a career in science, you would be well advised to do everything you can to develop his or her interest in music.

2.  *The following is excerpted from a new article from the* Weekly World News: *"First Photo of a Human Soul":*

What was expected to be a routine heart surgery wound up making religious and medical history when a photographer snapped a picture of the patient's body a split second after she died. The dramatic photo clearly shows a glowing angelic spirit rising up off the operating table as the line of Karin Fisher's heart monitor went flat at the moment of death. And while nobody in the operating theater actually saw the strange entity as it left the 32-year-old patient's body, scholars, clergymen and the Vatican itself are hailing the photo as the most dramatic proof of life after death ever.

"This is it. This is the proof that true believers the world over have been waiting for," Dr. Martin Muller, who has conducted an extensive study of the picture, told reporters.

Oddly enough, not one of the 12 doctors, nurses and technicians in the operating room saw the glowing spirit leave the woman's body, apparently because it wasn't visible to the naked eye.

But as a matter of routine the procedure was photographed by the hospital's director of education, Peter Valentin, who found a single black and white picture of the spirit among 72 prints that were made.

"The photo has been the focus of intense study and debate for several weeks now and the consensus of both scholars and clergymen is that it is indeed authentic," said Dr. Muller.

"That's not to say that there aren't any skeptics because there are," he continued.

"The problem with their position is that they can offer no alternative explanations for the flowing image that turned up on the picture. In fact, there are no alternative explanations. You either accept the image in faith, as I do, or you reject it. There is no in-between.[8]

3. To the editor: Dr. Richard Cannucci stated in a recent article in your paper that "current child psychology literature does not confirm the much-quoted connection between sugar and hyperactivity." Virtually every time I give my usually charming grandchildren a couple pieces of candy, they turn into pluperfect monsters. You understand, of course, I haven't done a prospective, randomized, double-blind study funded by a large federal grant to arrive at my conclusion.

4. *Graphologists claim to be able to tell a great deal about a person from their handwriting. The following is from a report prepared for the author by a professional graphologist:*

You are a person who is alive to the world about you and you react quickly, and in a friendly way to those who show you a friendly interest. You are easily influenced by life's many joys and sorrows, and your first response to any situation in life, pleasant or unpleasant, will be an emotionally responsive one. Even though you are strongly influenced by the way you feel, you will not go to extremes and allow your emotions to rule your life by controlling you entirely.

5. You have probably heard about back masking—inserting subliminal messages in recordings of popular music in reverse. If fact, some people claim that if you play such recordings backwards you can actually hear the message. But have you ever wondered how the mind deciphers the message, given that it hears it backwards? Well, the answer is quite simple. We do not hear individual words when we listen to speech or lyrics. Instead we hear whole sentences constructed, like a chain of linked metal loops, of the individual words. The whole sentences can be processed by the brain either forwards or backwards, much as a linked chain can be dragged back and forth.

6. Though most reports of UFOs can be explained in perfectly ordinary ways—sightings of weather balloons, blimps, the moon, etc.—there remains a small residue of cases which have no known explanation. These sightings are typically by reliable people and are often reported by a number of observers. Thus we can rule out the possibility of a hoax of some sort. It seems clear then that we have evidence that earth has been visited by beings from another planet or star system.

7.  *A professional psychic, Suzanne Jachius, said the following about her psychic impressions:*

I think the things I'm shown are the things we have some power over or choices in. So I report things in a way that gives people an opportunity to make some different choices. I'll say, "You're going to want to be careful about this." I can only believe that certain things need to happen, and us knowing about it isn't going to make any difference. What I've found is that I seem to look back about six months and look forward about a year—but it all looks like right now to me. I can't always differentiate. I have to leave that up to the client.[9]

8.  Is it just a coincidence that there are so many parallels between the lives of famous people living at different times? Perhaps. But perhaps not. It may be that we have lived past lives and that certain of our traits persist from lifetime to lifetime. You are no doubt aware of some of the eerie similarities between John F. Kennedy and Abraham Lincoln. This is only the tip of the iceberg. Consider the strange parallels between the lives of George Washington and Dwight Eisenhower:

1.  *Both came to prominence as victorious generals.*
2.  *Both served two full terms as president.*
3.  *Both gave famous farewell speeches warning the United States against foolish military policies.*
4.  *Both were replaced as president by Harvard graduates named John, from wealthy, prominent Massachusetts families.*
5.  *"Eisenhower" and "Washington" have ten letters each.*
6.  *"Dwight" and "George" have six letters each.*
7.  *Neither belonged to a political party before seeking the presidency.*

9.  "What goes around comes around." In this simple statement lies one of the most profound truths about human destiny, sometimes called the Law of Karma. Even the Bible recognizes this most fundamental of truths: "As ye sow, so shall ye reap." You may think there are bound to be exceptions to this cosmic law of justice. After all, people do not always suffer the consequences of the bad things they do nor are they consistently rewarded for the good. But have faith. The results of our actions may not catch up with us in this life, but there are other lives. What we sow in this existence, we may reap in another incarnation.

10. A recent study of 50 of America's most profitable companies revealed some interesting facts. Many of the companies have resisted the temptation to expand into new and unfamiliar industries. Or as Robert W. Johnson, former chairman of Johnson and Johnson, put it, "Never acquire a business you don't know how to run." It seems clear that the odds increase that a large company will remain profitable over the long haul if it sticks to doing business in areas with which it is familiar.

11. Some psychics claim to be able to help police with cases usually involving missing persons or unsolved murders. These "psychic detectives" claim that they "work with" police departments as "consultants" on many of

their unsolved cases. Typically, a psychic will go to the scene of a crime or the place where a person was last seen before disappearing and will "see," using ESP, important facts pertaining to the case. In fact, there are very few instances in which the police initiate a request for help from a psychic. In most cases, the parents or relatives of a missing or dead person contact a psychic, pay for their help, and then offer their findings to the local police department.

*Exercises 12–14 are all taken from Bio-Rhythm—A Personal Science.[10] Biorhythm is the notion that from birth to death each of us is influenced by three internal cycles—the physical, the emotional, and the intellectual.*

12. On the evening of November 11, 1960, a retired Swiss importer named George Thommen was interviewed on the "Long John Nebel Show," a radio talkathon based in New York City. What Thommen had to say sounded surprising to most people and incredible to some. However, the strangest thing Thommen said was in the form of a warning. He cautioned that Clark Gable, who was then in the hospital recovering from a heart attack suffered six days before while filming *The Misfits* with Marilyn Monroe, would have to be very careful on November 16. On that date, explained Thommen, Gable's "physical rhythm" would be "critical." As a result, his condition would be unstable, putting him in danger of a relapse.

    Few listeners took Thommen's warning seriously. Gable and his doctors were probably unaware of it. On Wednesday, November 16, 1960, Clark Gable suffered an unexpected second heart attack and died. His doctor later admitted that his life might have been saved if the needed medical equipment had been in place beside his bed when he was stricken a second time.

13. Actually, the theory of biorhythm is little more than an extension and generalization of the enormous amount of research that scientists have already done on the many biological rhythms and cycles of life. From the migration of swallows and the feeding patterns of oysters to the levels of hormones in human blood and the patterns of sleep, life can be defined as regulated time. Countless rhythms, most of them fairly predictable, can be found in even the simplest of our bodily functions. Even the smallest component of our bodies, the cell, follows several clearly defined cycles as it creates and uses up energy.

14. There is nothing in biorhythm theory that contradicts scientific knowledge. . . . But until we can perform strictly controlled studies of how and why biorhythm works, and until many other researchers have been able to replicate these studies, we will have to base the case for biorhythm on purely empirical research. . . . Ultimately, however, the most convincing studies of biorhythm are those you can do yourself. By working out your own biorhythm chart and biorhythm profiles for particular days, and then comparing them with your experiences of up and down days, of illness and health,

of success and failure, you will be able to judge for yourself.

15. For years, stories have been circulating about an internal combustion engine, invented sometime in the 1950s, that burns a simple combination of hydrogen and oxygen, instead of gasoline. This "water engine" as it is sometimes called, could revolutionize the world economy by freeing us of our dependence on fossil fuels and making transportation virtually free to everyone. But don't hold your breath. The major players in the global economy are a tight confederation of industries and countries involved in the manufacture, maintenance, and fueling of automobiles. So enormous is the global monetary investment in the status quo that it is virtually impossible that the water engine will even see the light of day. The major oil and automotive companies have seen to it that all patents pertaining to this revolutionary new invention are under their control and they have orchestrated the suppression of all information about this incredible new invention that would, if marketed, cost them billions of dollars. Ask any representative of the oil or automotive industry— or any government official for that matter—about the water engine and I predict this is just what you will hear: either "no comment" or "there's simply no such thing."

16. *The following newspaper article appeared under the heading, "Ex-USO Professor Theorizes About Alien Beings:"*

Aliens from distant worlds maybe watching earth and making unofficial contact with selected humans, says a recently retired scientist at Oregon State University. His theory is that advanced and benevolent space beings may have adopted an embargo on official contact with earthlings, wishing to avoid the chaos that could sweep the planet if their presence were suddenly revealed.

Instead, they have adopted a "leaky embargo" policy that allows contact only with citizens whose stories are unlikely to be credible to scientists and the government, said the scientist, James W. Deardorff, 58, professor emeritus of atmospheric sciences.

"They just want to let those know who are prepared to accept it in their minds that there are other beings," Deardorff said. "They may want to slowly prepare us for the shock that could come later when they reveal themselves. . . ."

Deardorff is prepared to accept many ideas looked upon skeptically by other scientists, including telepathy and the possibility of time travel and physical dimensions other than space and time.

His open-mindedness has made it more difficult to operate in the scientific mainstream, where scientific committees have been formed to debunk theories about UFOs and psychic phenomena.

"There's a lot of polarization going on now," he said, adding that he has had trouble getting some papers on extraterrestrials published in scientific journals. "There's a lot less middle ground than there used to be," he said. "It's no accident that I'm getting more active in this area now after retirement."[11]

17. I have a new theory about that most mysterious of forces, gravity. Though physicists can de-

scribe for us the laws which gravity follows, they have failed entirely to explain the mechanism by which gravity works. I think I have the answer. Every massive object in the universe generates invisible, spring-like tendrils in the direction of every other object in its immediate vicinity. When these tendrils connect, they function like a coiled spring, with the tension varying in direct proportion to the product of the masses of the objects they connect and in inverse proportion to the square of the distance between the objects. I call these tendrils "virtual springs." Thus, virtual springs grow in strength as objects are closer together and weaken as objects recede from one another. That I am on to something remarkable is suggested by the following. If my virtual spring theory is right, objects of differing masses should all accelerate toward another massive object, say, the surface of the earth, and, moreover, should do so at roughly the same rate. By careful experimentation I have established the truth of both these predictions. Massive objects all tend to fall toward the earth and tend to do so at precisely the same rate of acceleration, irrespective of mass!

18. Telekinesis is the ability to bring about physical changes by purely mental processes. Is telekinesis for real? Consider the following experiment. A computer is programmed to generate numbers at random. When an odd number is generated, the computer prints out "odd," and when an even number is generated, it prints out "even." An experimenter instructs the computer to proceed, one number at a time. Prior to the generation of each number, an experimental subject is instructed to think "odd" or "even" and then to mark down their choice on a tally sheet. The experimenter then instructs the computer to generate a number and the result is tallied against the choice of the experimental subject. Several hundred trials are run in this way. Under these experimental conditions, it is predicted that subjects with telekinetic ability will score much higher than chance would predict, i.e., the computer and the experimental subject will agree more than 50 percent of the time.

19. Recently, I carried out a telepathy experiment on 50 of my students. I shuffled a standard deck of playing cards. Sitting behind a screen that blocked me from my subject's line of sight, I turned over the cards one at a time. I would concentrate on the value of the care—ace, three, king, etc.—and then instruct the subjects to record what they thought the card was. I did this for the entire deck. Now, simply guessing, we would expect someone to get about 8 percent right (1/13). And indeed, none of my subjects scored much higher or lower than this. But that is not the end of the story! Close analysis of the results shows that several students were within two cards of the card I was concentrating on nearly half the time! It seems clear to me that these subjects have demonstrated at least some ability to pick up thoughts telepathically.

20.   *From a flyer advertising a chiropractic clinic:*

Ronald Pero, Ph.D., researched the immune system at the University of Lund Medical School, Lund, Sweden, and the Preventative Medical Institute, New York City. He measured both immune resistance to disease and the ability to repair genetic damage.

In a news report about his study in *East/West Journal,* November 1989, chiropractic patients were compared to two groups: normal, healthy people, and cancer patients. The chiropractic patients were all in long term care on a wellness basis. Their immune function was measured to be two times stronger than the healthy people, and four times stronger than the sick! And this increase occurred regardless of age. With ongoing chiropractic care, the immune system does not deteriorate, as in other groups.

21.   *From an ad for past life drawings— drawings by a psychic of the way we looked in our past lives:*

Since I've been doing Past Life Drawings and Readings for people, I'm often amazed at how relevant the information is in their present lives. Even though we may have had thousands of incarnations, I've found that there are usually three main past lives which are influencing our present lives the most.

One woman that I did drawings for had a past life in India as a young male who rode and trained elephants to lift logs and move stones to build a temple. Years later when the temple was completed, the man decided to spend the rest of his life meditating in the temple. The woman revealed that she had been doing Eastern meditation for many years and she also had a large ceramic elephant lamp, elephant bookends and other elephant figurines all around the house.

One man had an unpleasant life on a ship which ended when he was tied and thrown overboard into the ocean and drowned. The man had always been afraid of water in this life and never learned to swim. I worked with this man to bring the drowning experience into the present time and helped him to release the emotions and fear connected with it. A month later he was swimming and innertubing in Timothy Lake with his wife and sons.

22.   Many strange and wonderful things are attributed to the mysterious power of the pyramid. For example, you can increase the life of a razor blade by keeping it stored inside a simple plastic pyramid. If you don't believe me, try this simple experiment. After you use your razor, remove the blade, wash it in warm water and then dry the blade off. Finally, place it inside or under a small pyramid-shaped container. I think you will be surprised at how long the blade retains its sharpness.

23.   If you are wondering how pyramids manage to accomplish this marvelous feat, consider the following explanation by G. Patrick Flannigen, self-proclaimed pyramid power expert: The shape of the pyramid acts as a sort of lens or focus for the transmission of bio-cosmic energy.

24.   A recent study has shown that, on average, a graduate of an ivy league college will make more money over the course of his or her career than a graduate of any other college. Moreover, a graduate of an east coast college

will make more than a graduate of a midwestern, southern, or western college. It seems clear that if you want to make it financially, you ought to try to get into an ivy league school and, if you can't get in, at least go to college on the east coast.

25. *The following newspaper story appeared under the headline, "Gyroscope Test Possibly Defies Gravity:"*

Japanese scientists have reported that small gyroscopes lose weight when spun under certain conditions, apparently in defiance of gravity. If proved correct, the finding would mark a stunning scientific advance, but experts said they doubted that it would survive intense scrutiny.

A systematic way to negate gravitation, the attraction between all masses and particles of matter in the universe, has eluded scientists since the principles of the force were first elucidated by Issac Newton in the 17th century. The anti-gravity work is reported in the Dec. 18, 1989 issue of *Physical Review Letters,* which is regarded by experts as one of the world's leading journals of physics and allied fields. Its articles are rigorously reviewed by other scientists before being accepted for publication, and it rejects far more than it accepts.

Experts who have seen the report said that it seemed to be based on sound research and appeared to have no obvious sources of experimental error, but they cautioned that other seemingly reliable reports have collapsed under close examination.

The work was performed by Hideo Hayasaka and Sakae Takeuchi of the engineering faculty at Tohoku University in Sendai, Japan.

Unlike the exaggerated claims made for low-temperature or "cold" nuclear fusion this year, the current results are presented with scientific understatement. The authors do not claim to have defied gravity, but simply say their results "cannot be explained by the usual theories."

"It's an astounding claim," said Robert L. Park, a professor of physics at the University of Maryland who is director of the Washington office of the American Physical Society, which publishes *Physical Review Letters.* "It would be revolutionary if true. But it's almost certainly wrong. Almost all extraordinary claims are wrong."

The experiment looked at weight changes in spinning gyroscopes whose rotors weighed 140 and 176 grams, or 5 and 6.3 ounces. When the gyroscopes were spun clockwise, as viewed from above, the researchers found no change in their weight. But when spun counterclockwise, they appeared to lose weight.[12]

26. It seems that children who spend more time watching popular programs on commercial television tend to be lower achievers in school. Several studies have established that performance on standardized tests varies in inverse proportion to the amount of television a child under the age of 12 watches. The more television of this sort a child watches, the lower are his or her scores likely to be.

27. *Nostradamus, a sixteenth century French physician, is said to have predicted with great accuracy things that occurred long after his death. Nostradamus' prophecies were written as short poems, called quatrains. The following are said to foretell recent events:*

One burned, not dead, but apoplectical, Shall be found to have eaten up his hands,

When the city shall damn the heretical man,
Who as they thought had changed their laws.
   To the great empire, quite another shall come,
Being distant from goodness and happiness,
Governed by one of base parentage
The kingdom shall fall, a great unhappiness.

> A prominent Nostradamus scholar gives the following interpretations. The first quatrain refers to President Nixon's downfall and the Watergate scandal. The second is said to predict the rise and dominance of communism and the subsequent subjugation of the Western democracies.[13]

28.  *From a flyer headed "Does Sunday School Make a Difference?":*

Max Juken lived in New York. He did not believe in religious training. He refused to take his children to church, even when they asked to go. He has had 1,062 descendants; 300 were sent to prison for an average term of 13 years; 190 were prostitutes; 680 were admitted alcoholics. His family, thus far, has cost the state in excess of $420,000. They made no contribution to society.

   Jonathan Edwards lived in the same state, at the same time as the Jukes. He saw that his children were in church every Sunday. He had 929 descendants, of these 430 were ministers; 86 became college professors; 13 became university presidents; 75 authored good books; five were elected to the United States Congress, and two to the Senate. One was Vice-President of his nation. His family never cost the state one cent, but has contributed to the life of plenty in this land today.

29.  Some dentists and "alternative" medical practitioners believe we are being poisoned by mercury contained in our dental fillings. When we chew, minute quantities of mercury are released from our fillings and are ingested into the body. Over time, the amount of mercury in the body is liable to reach toxic proportions. A flyer on mercury toxicity and dental fillings gives the following as symptoms related to mercury poisoning and suggest that if you have more than a few, you ought to carefully consider having you mercury amalgam filling removed:

| | |
|---|---|
| Anxiety | Apathy |
| Confusion | Depression |
| Emotional instability | Fits of anger |
| Irritability | Nervousness |
| Nightmares | Tension |
| High blood pressure | Low blood pressure |
| Chronic headaches | Dizziness |
| Muscle twitches | Ringing in ears |
| Colds hands or feet | Decreased sexual activity |
| Leg cramps | Pain in joints |
| Weight loss | Fatigue |
| Drowsiness | Lack of energy |
| Allergies | Over-sleeping |
| Bad breath | Bleeding gums |
| Acne | Rough skin |
| Skin flushes | Unexplained skin rashes |

30.  Dear Ann Landers: In a recent column, you recounted how Reader's Digest tested the honesty of Europeans by dropping wallets in various cities. You

wondered how the United States would fare if put to the same test. Well, we can tell you. WE did some U.S. testing and printed the results in the December 1995 issue. Here's a copy.

Lesta Cordil

Public Relations Associate Director, *Reader's Digest.*

Dear Lesta: Many thanks for the assist. I'm sure my readers will find the results interesting. I certainly did. Readers, if you're wondering how your city stacked up (I thought Chicago would have done very well), you might not find the answer here. The experiment was done in only 12 cities. Here's how it was set up:

One hundred and twenty wallets containing $50 each were dropped on the streets and in the shopping malls, restaurants, gas stations and office buildings in a number of U.S. cities. In each wallet was a name, local address, phone number, family pictures and coupons, as well as the cash. A *Reader's Digest* reporter followed on the heels of the wallet-croppers, and this is what his research revealed.

Of the 120 wallets dropped, 80 were returned with all the money intact. Seattle turned out to be the most honest city. Nine of the ten wallets dropped in Seattle were returned with the $50 inside.

Three smaller cities turned out to be very near the top for honesty; Meadville, Pa.; Concord, N.H.; and Cheyenne, Wyo. In each of these cities eight wallets were returned and two were not.

St. Louis came in next—of the ten wallets dropped, seven were returned and three were kept. The suburbs of Boston ties with St. Louis. The suburbs of Los Angeles were not quite as honest. Six wallets were returned, four were kept. Four cities—Las Vegas; Dayton, Ohio; Atlanta; and the suburbs of Houston - shared the poorest records. Five wallets were returned and five were kept.

Small towns scored 80 percent returns and proved to be more honest than larger cities, with the exception of Seattle. Women, it turned out, were more honest than men - 72 percent to 62 percent. Young people posted a 67 percent return rate - the same as the overall average.[14]

## A SOLUTION TO EXERCISE 1

*The suggestion in this passage is that there is some sort of causal connection between an interest in science and an interest in music. The facts about Einstein and Newton are most likely meant to imply a correlation between the two, though the passage does not come right out and say that a higher percentage of scientists than nonscientists are interested in music. Otherwise there would be no reason to believe that a child's interest in music would lead him or her to pursue a career in science rather than something*

*else. Now, even if such a correlation could be established, serious questions could be raised about its significance. There are a number of ways of explaining such a correlation short of suggesting that an interest in music causes one to become interested in a career in science.*

*The real problem with the passage, however, is that it involves the fallacy we have called "False Anomalies." We are told of two instances in which well known scientists have shown an interest in music. The crucial facts omitted, of course, are those about scientists generally. Do we have any reason to believe that what we learn about Einstein and Newton are true of scientists generally or of more scientists than* *nonscientists? Lacking this information, the causal claim made in the passage must be understood to be wholly unfounded.*

## NOTES

1. For a excellent account of the history of phlogiston theory and discussion of its philosophical implications, see *The Theory of Science: An Introduction to the History, Logic and Philosophy of Science,* by George Gale. (New York, McGraw-Hill, 1979.) I am indebted to Gale for the discussion of phlogiston in the text.

2. This is not to say that mainstream scientists do not on occasion engage in fallacious reasoning and even worse. For more on this topic, see *Betrayers of Truth: Fraud and Deceit in Science,* by Broad and Wade. (London: Oxford University Press, 1982.)

3. Raymond A. Moody, *Life After Life* (New York: Bantam Books, 1975), pp. 21–22.

4. This phrase was coined by John Stuart Mill (1806–1873) in *A System of Logic,* one of the first comprehensive studies on the ways in which causal connections are established.

5. For a good review of the controversy surrounding the work of Duesberg and Root-Bernstein see "Special Section—The AIDS Heresies," in *Skeptic,* Vol. 3, No. 2, 1995.

6. The National Science Foundation reports that out of about 18,000 grants made in 1991, only 52 cases of misconduct were reported. On a more distressing note, however, a survey done that year by the National Association for the Advancement of Science of 1,500 scientists revealed the following. More than a quarter of the respondents said they had witnessed faking, falsifying, or outright theft of research in the past decade.

7. P.B. Medawar, *The Limits of Science* (New York, Harper and Row, 1984) pg.87.

8. Donald Rivers, "First Photo of a Human Soul," *Weekly World News,* Sept. 15, 1992.

9. Jill Spitznass, "A Woman's Intuition," *The Portland Tribune,* April 30, 2002.

10. Gittelson, Bernard, *Bio-Rhthym: A Personal Science,* (New York: Warner Books, 1975) pp. 15-19.

11. John Hayes, "Ex-OSU Professor Theorizes About Alien Beings," *The Oregonian,* Jan. 18, 1987. Reprinted by permission of the author.

12. Copyright 1989 by the New York Times Company. Reprinted by permission. This experiment was replicated a year and a half later by two physicists at Tokyo University. (See "Observation Against the Weight Reduction in Spinning Gyroscopes," by A. Imanishi, K. Maruyama, S. Midorikawa, and T. Morimote, in *Journal of the Physical Society of Japan,* Vol.60, no. 4, April, 1991). They detected no weight change due to the rotation of their gyroscopes. Since then no further reports of research on this phenomenon has surfaced in the scientific literature. Do you sense a conspiracy here?

13. Adopted from *The Complete Prophesies of Nostradamus,* translated, edited, and interpreted by Henry C. Roberts (New York: Nostradamus Company, 1982).

14. "Dear Ann Landers," in *The Oregonian,* November 24, 1996.

# Further Reading

## Scientific Method and the Philosophy of Science

Elster, Jon. *Nuts and Bolts for the Social Sciences.* Cambridge: Cambridge University Press, 1989.

Gale, George. *Theory of Science: An Introduction to the History, Logic and Philosophy of Science.* New York: McGraw-Hill, 1979.

Giere, Ronald N. *Understanding Scientific Reasoning.* (3rd ed.) New York: Holt, Reinhart and Winston, 1991.

Hacking, Ian. *Representing and Intervening: Introductory Topics in the Philosophy of Natural Science.* Cambridge: Cambridge University Press, 1983.

Hempel, Carl G. *The Philosophy of Natural Science.* Englewood Cliffs, N.J.: Prentice-Hall, 1966.

Homans, George C. *The Nature of a Social Science.* New York: Harcourt, Brace & World, 1967.

Huck, Schulyer W., and Sandler, Howard M. *Rival Hypotheses: Alternative Interpretations of Data Based Conclusions.* New York: Harper and Row, 1979.

Kuhn, Thomas S. *The Structure of Scientific Revolutions.* (2nd ed.) Chicago: University of Chicago Press, 1970.

Medawar, P.B. *The Limits of Science.* New York: Harper and Row, 1984.

Moore, Kathleen Dean. *A Field Guide to Inductive Arguments.* (2nd ed.) Dubuque: Kendall/Hunt, 1989.

Popper, Karl R. *The Logic of Scientific Discovery.* (2nd rev. ed.) New York: Harper Torchbooks, 1968.

Salmon, Merrilee H., et al. *Introduction to the Philosophy of Science.* Englewood Cliffs, N.J.: Prentice-Hall, 1992.

Toulmin, Stephen. *The Philosophy of Science: An Introduction.* New York: Harper and Row, 1960.

## Pseudoscience

Abell, G.O. and Singer, B. *Science and the Paranormal.* New York: Scribner, 1981.

Broad, William, and Wade, Nichola. *Betrayers of the Truth: Fraud and Deceit in Science.* Oxford: Oxford University Press, 1982.

Friedlander, Michael W. *At the Fringes of Science.* Boulder: Westview Press, 1998.

Gardner, Martin. *Fads and Fallacies in the Name of Science.* New York: Dover Publications, 1957.

_____. *Science: Good, Bad and Bogus.* Buffalo: Prometheus, 1981.

Glymour, Clark, and Stalker, Douglas. *Examining Holistic Medicine.* Buffalo: Prometheus, 1985.

Gray, Willian D. *Thinking Critically about the New Age.* Belmont: Wadsworth Publishing Company, 1991.

Harris, Sidney. *Quantum Leaps in the Wrong Direction.* Washington D.C.: Joseph Henry Press, 2001.

Hines, Terence. *Pseudo-science and the Paranormal.* Buffalo: Prometheus, 1988.

Hyman, Ray. *The Elusive Quarry: A Scientific Appraisal of Psychical Research.* Buffalo: Prometheus, 1989.

*National Council Against Health Fraud Newsletter,* Box 1276, Loma Linda, CA., 92354.

Park, Robert. *Voodoo Science.* New York: Oxford University Press, 2000.

Radner, Daisie, and Michael. *Science and Unreason.* Belmont: Wadsworth Publishing Company, 1982.

Randi, James. *Flim-Flam! The Truth about Unicorns, Parapsychology and Other Delusions.* New York: Thomas Y. Crowell, 1980.

Sagan, Carl. *The Demon-Haunted World: Science as a Candle in the Dark.* New York: Random House, 1996.

Schlick, Theodore Jr., and Vaughn, Lewis. *How to Think About Weird Things.* (3rd ed.) New York: McGraw-Hill, 2002.

Shultz, Ted, ed. *The Fringes of Reason: A Whole Earth Catalogue.* New York: Harmony Books, 1989.

*Skeptic Magazine.* P.O. Box 338, Altedena, CA 91001.

*The Skeptical Enquirer.* Box 229, Buffalo, N.Y. 14215-0229.

# Index